GCSE German
VOCABULARY

Michael Buckby with Kate Corney

Heinemann

Heinemann Educational Publishers, Halley Court, Jordan Hill, Oxford OX2 8EJ
A division of Reed Educational & Professional Publishing Limited

OXFORD   FLORENCE   PRAGUE   MADRID   ATHENS   MELBOURNE   AUCKLAND
KUALA LUMPUR   SINGAPORE   TOKYO   IBADAN   NAIROBI   KAMPALA
JOHANNESBURG   GABORONE   PORTSMOUTH NH (USA)   CHICAGO
MEXICO CITY   SAO PAOLO

00 99 98 97 96
10 9 8 7 6 5 4 3 2 1

A catalogue record is available for this book from the British Library on request.

ISBN 0 435 37860 0

Produced by Goodfellow & Egan

Photographs were provided by Kate Corney

Printed and bound in Great Britain by Bath Press

CONTENTS

◀ *How to use this book* ▶

This book contains all the words and phrases you need to learn in order to do well in your German exam. In some exams you may use a dictionary but if you know your key vocabulary and key phrases you will be able to work faster and complete all the questions in the time available.

The words and phrases are presented topic by topic. There are two sections – Foundation and Higher. If you are taking GCSE Higher tier you should learn both sections. If you are taking GCSE Foundation tier you should concentrate on the Foundation section.

Verbs are given in the infinitive form.

How to learn

Your learning will be much more effective and easy if you follow a few simple rules.

● Start several months before your exam: don't leave it to a last minute rush!

● Have regular and short learning sessions: three times 20 minutes each week is excellent, and better than one session of an hour.

● Before you begin a new topic, always go back and test yourself on the topics you have already learnt. In this way, you won't forget them.

● When you learn, it is essential to use your brain actively. Do not just sit and read the words: do things with the words which will help you to understand and remember them. The activities below can be used with any list. Try several of them with each list until you have learnt all the words in it.

Activities to help you learn

Learning the words

● Try to learn eight to ten words. Then cover the English and look at the German. Write the English equivalents and then compare what you have written with the book. Continue until you get them all right.

● Learn eight to ten words. Then cover the German and look at the English. Write the German equivalents and say the words to yourself as you write them. Then compare your list with the book. Continue until you get them all right.

● People tend to learn best the words at the start and finish of lists. To learn the words in the middle, re-write the lists and put the words in the middle at the top or bottom of your list.

● As you look at the list, write any words you are finding difficult to learn, omitting all the vowels (e.g. Rücken - Rckn, Gesicht - Gscht). Close your book and, looking only at your shorthand notes, write all the words in full.

- Make up a 'word-sun' as you look at a list. Write a key word in the middle and other words which relate to it at the end of each 'ray', e.g.

Give yourself 30 seconds to 'photograph' this in your mind. Then cover up your 'word-sun' and try to write an exact copy of it. Compare it with the original.

Learning the sentences

When you are confident that you know all the words, work on the model sentences. These are sentences which you could use in your exam and gain high marks for. Here are some activities to help you learn them.

- Try to learn six to eight sentences. Then write the first letter only of each word. Close your book and try to say, and then write, all the sentences in full. Check with the book and continue until you get them all right.

- As above, but writing just the first and last words of each sentence as your guide, plus the number of missing words. So, for "Die Schule ist um halb vier aus" you write "Die —— aus"(5).

- Copy any sentences in the list which are true for you or your school or town, etc. Then change the other sentences so that they are true for you. So, for example, if your favourite lesson is music, you would write "Musik" instead of "Mathe" in this sentence: "Mein Lieblingsfach ist Mathe, weil es einfach ist".

- Use a ruler to cover up parts of some sentences when you think you know them. Then see if you can fill in the gaps. You can cover sentences in different ways:

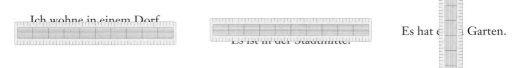

- For any sentences which you find hard to learn, write the English on one side of a small card or piece of paper, and the German on the other side. Keep these in a pocket or bag. Whenever you have a few minutes free, look at them in any order. If you look at the English, say the German to yourself and then look at the other side and check. If you look at the German first, say the English to yourself and then check. Then shuffle the cards and do it again.

- You could make similar sets of cards, e.g.
  - write a question on one side and the answer on the other.
  - draw a picture on one side to illustrate the German sentence on the other side.
  - time yourself working on a set of cards and then try to improve on that time.

FOUNDATION TIER

EVERYDAY ACTIVITIES

◀ *Language of the classroom* ▶

Classroom instructions

antworten	to answer	**der Kassetten-**	cassette recorder
arbeiten	to work	**rekorder (-)**	
aufhören	to stop	**das Kreuz (-e)**	cross
aufmachen	to open	**das Papier**	paper
aufpassen	to pay attention	**der Partner (-)**	partner (male)
aufschlagen	to open	**die Partnerin (-nen)**	partner (female)
kopieren	to copy	**die Tafel (-n)**	blackboard
lesen	to read	**der Tageslicht-**	Overhead projector
sagen	to say	**projektor (-en)**	
sehen	to see	**der Test**	test
vergessen	to forget	**das Wörterbuch**	dictionary
zuhören	to listen	**(¨er)**	
zumachen	to close	**doch**	yes (you use this
die Aufgabe	exercise		when the person you
das Beispiel (-e)	example		are talking to expects
das Buch (¨er)	book		you to say "no".)
der Haken	tick	**fertig**	ready
das Heft (-e)	exercise book	**ja**	yes
		nein	no

Sag es auf deutsch, bitte.	Say it in German, please.
Macht eure Bücher auf.	Open your books.
Hast du dein Heft vergessen?	Have you forgotten your exercise book?
Arbeite mit einem Partner.	Work with a partner.
Seid ihr fertig?	Have you finished?
Wer kann antworten?	Who can answer?
Paßt gut auf.	Pay attention.

Make classroom requests

der Bleistift (-e)	pencil	**der Stift (-e)**	pen
die Haus-	homework	**der Kugel-**	biro; pen (this can be
aufgaben		**schreiber (-)**	shortened to "der
das Lineal (-e)	ruler		Kuli")
die Mappe (-n)	school bag	**fragen**	to ask
die Seite (-n)	side; page		

Ich habe keinen Bleistift.	I haven't got a pencil.
Ich habe mein Buch vergessen.	I've forgotten my book.
Hast du einen Kuli?	Have you got a pen?
Ich habe meine Hausaufgaben nicht gemacht.	I haven't done my homework.

Say if you (don't) understand

die Antwort (-en)	answer	**verstehen**	to understand
die Frage (-n)	question		

Verstehst du das?	Do you understand?
Nein, ich verstehe es nicht.	No, I don't understand.
Ich habe die Hausaufgaben nicht verstanden.	I didn't understand the homework.

Ask someone to repeat

wiederholen	to repeat	**nochmal**	again

Wie bitte?	Pardon?
Könnten Sie bitte die Frage wiederholen?	Would you repeat the question, please?
Was haben Sie gesagt?	What did you say?
Können Sie das nochmal sagen?	Can you say that again?

Ask someone to spell a word

buchstabieren	to spell	**schreiben**	to write

Wie schreibt man es?	How do you write it?
Können Sie es buchstabieren?	Can you spell it?

Here is the German alphabet with a guide to how the letters are pronounced:

A	like <u>ar</u> in are	O	like <u>ow</u> in low
B	like <u>bay</u>	P	like <u>pea</u> in peasant
C	like <u>tsay</u>	Q	like <u>koo</u>
D	like <u>day</u>	R	like <u>air</u>
E	like <u>ay</u> in day	S	like <u>ess</u>
F	like <u>eff</u>	T	like <u>tay</u>
G	like <u>gay</u>	U	like <u>oo</u> in do
H	like <u>ha</u>	V	like <u>fow</u> to rhyme
I	like <u>ea</u> in tea		with cow
J	like <u>yacht</u>	W	like <u>vay</u>
K	like <u>car</u>	X	like <u>eeks</u>
L	like <u>ell</u>	Y	like <u>üpsilon</u>
M	like <u>emm</u>	Z	like <u>tset</u>
N	like <u>enn</u>		

Ask if someone speaks German or English

Deutsch	German	**die Fremd-**	foreign language
Englisch	English	**sprache (-n)**	
sprechen	to speak		

Sprechen Sie Deutsch?	Do you speak German?
Er spricht kein Englisch.	He doesn't speak English.

Ask what things are called and what words mean

bedeuten	to mean	**heißen**	to be called

Was bedeutet es auf englisch?	What does that mean in English?
Wie heißt es auf deutsch?	What is it in German?
Wie sagt man das auf deutsch?	How do you say that in German?

Say you do not know

die Ahnung (-en)	idea	**wissen**	to know

Ich weiß es nicht.	I don't know.
Ich habe keine Ahnung.	I've no idea.

Say if something is correct

der Fehler (-)	error	**stimmen**	to be right
bestimmt	definitely; of course	**Stimmt das?**	Is that right?
falsch	wrong	**Ja, bestimmt.**	Yes, of course.
richtig	right	**Das stimmt nicht.**	That's not right.

◀ *School* ▶

Express opinions about school

das Fach (¨er)	subject	**alt**	old
der Lehrer (-)	teacher (male)	**einfach**	easy
die Lehrerin (-nen)	teacher (female)	**groß**	big
das Lieblingsfach (¨er)	favourite subject	**modern**	modern
die Note (-n)	mark	**schwer**	hard
es gefällt mir	I like it	**wichtig**	important
ich mag	I like	**besonders**	special; particularly
		weil	because

Die Schule gefällt mir sehr.	I like school very much.
Ich mag meine Schule, weil sie modern ist.	I like my school because it's modern.
Ich mag meine Schule nicht. Sie ist zu groß.	I don't like my school. It's too large.
Mein Lieblingsfach ist Mathe, weil es einfach ist.	My favourite subject is Maths because it's easy.
Ich mag Kunst nicht, weil es schwer ist.	I don't like art because it's hard.
Geschichte gefällt mir besonders gut, weil ich gute Noten bekomme.	I particularly like history because I get good marks.

School subjects and facilities

Die Fächer	School subjects		Mathe (Mathematik)	Maths
Biologie	Biology		Musik	Music
Chemie	Chemistry		Naturwissenschaft	Science
Drama	Drama		Physik	Physics
Englisch	English		Religion	R.E.
Erdkunde	Geography		Sozialkunde	social science
Französisch	French		Spanisch	Spanish
Geographie	Geography		Sport	Sport
Geschichte	History		Technik	Technology
Informatik	Information technology		Turnen	P.E.
Kunst	Art		Werken	Technology; craft

die Gesamtschule (-n)	comprehensive school
das Gymnasium (Gymnasien)	grammar school
die Hauptschule (-n)	secondary modern school
die Realschule (-n)	secondary technical school
die Schule (-n)	school
der Schuldirektor (-)	headteacher (male)
die Schuldirektorin (-nen)	headteacher (female)
die Bibliothek (-en)	library
die Klasse (-n)	class
das Klassenzimmer (-)	classroom
die Turnhalle (-n)	sports hall
besuchen	to visit; go to (a school)

Wir haben Englisch und Französisch.	We do English and French.
Am Montag haben wir Erdkunde.	We have geography on Monday.
Ich besuche eine Gesamtschule.	I go to a comprehensive school.
Wir haben eine große Turnhalle.	We've got a large sports hall.
Wir haben eine neue Bibliothek.	We've got a new library.

Travel to and from school

das Auto (-s)	car		kommen	to come
der Bus (-se)	bus		zurückkommen	to come back
das Fahrrad (¨er)	bike		bequem	comfortable
das Rad (¨er)	bike		zu Fuß	on foot
der Wagen (-)	car; vehicle		heute morgen	this morning
fahren	to go; travel			

Wie kommst du zur Schule?	How do you come to school?
Ich komme zu Fuß zur Schule.	I walk to school.

Im Winter fahre ich mit dem Bus.	I go by bus in the winter.
Heute morgen bin ich mit dem Rad zur Schule gekommen.	I came to school by bike this morning.
Gewöhnlich komme ich mit dem Auto, weil es bequemer ist.	I normally come by car because it's more comfortable.

Welche Fächer hat Claudia am Montag? Schreib die Buchstaben von den richtigen Bildern.

	Montag
7.30	Geschichte
8.20	Englisch
PAUSE	
9.20	Kunst
10.10	Kunst
GROßE PAUSE	
11.20	Mathe
12.50	Erdkunde

a
b
c
d
e
f
g
h
i

When school begins and ends

beginnen	to begin
enden	to end
die Stunde (-n)	lesson
der Stundenplan	time-table

endlich	finally
erst	first
letzte	last

Wann beginnt die Schule?	When does school begin?
Die Schule beginnt um acht Uhr fünfzig.	School begins at eight fifty.
Die erste Stunde beginnt um zwanzig nach neun.	The first lesson starts at twenty past nine.
Wann ist die Schule aus?	When does school end?
Die Schule ist um halb vier aus.	School ends at half past three.

Lessons: how many there are and how long they last

die Doppel-stunde (-n)	double lesson	der Unterricht	teaching; lesson
		dauern	to last
die Einzel-stunde (-n)	single lesson	lang	long
		langweilig	boring
die Minute (-n)	minute	(am) Tag	(in a) day

Wie viele Stunden hast du am Tag?	How many lessons do you have in a day?
Wir haben fünf Stunden am Tag.	We have five lessons a day.
Wie lange dauert eine Stunde?	How long does a lesson last?
Eine Einzelstunde dauert fünfzig Minuten.	A single lesson lasts fifty minutes.
Ich finde das zu lang, weil es langweilig wird.	I find that too long, because it gets boring.

Some important numbers

zehn	10	fünfzig	50
fünfzehn	15	sechzig	60
zwanzig	20	siebzig	70
fünfundzwanzig	25	achtzig	80
dreißig	30	neunzig	90
vierzig	40	hundert	100

Breaktimes and lunchtimes

die Kantine (-n)	canteen	die Pause (-n)	break
die Mittags-pause (-n)	lunch break	(am) Nachmittag	(in the) afternoon
		(am) Vormittag	(in the) morning
nach Hause	(to go) home	es gibt	there is
essen	to eat	haben	to have
gehen	to go		

Wann beginnt die Mittagspause?	When does the midday break begin?
Um zwölf Uhr.	At midday.
Was machst du?	What do you do?
Ich esse in der Kantine.	I eat in the school canteen.
Ich gehe manchmal nach Hause.	I sometimes go home.
Ich mache meine Hausaufgaben.	I do my homework.
Wie viele Pausen gibt es am Tag?	How many breaks are there in a day?
Wir haben eine Pause am Vormittag und eine kurze Pause am Nachmittag.	We have a break in the morning and a short break in the afternoon.

Extra-curricular activities

der Austausch	exchange visit	fernsehen	to watch television
die Klassen-fahrt (-en)	class trip	hören	to listen to
		Sport treiben	to do sport

Was machst du, wenn du nicht in der Schule bist?	What do you do when you're not at school?
Ich höre Musik.	I listen to music.
Ich treibe gern Sport.	I like to do sport.
Ich sehe fern.	I watch television.
Letztes Jahr habe ich einen Austausch gemacht.	Last year I went on a school exchange.
Wir machen nächste Woche eine Klassenfahrt.	We are doing a class trip next week.

Homework

die Prüfung	exam		**gewöhnlich**	usually
lernen	to learn		**jeden Abend**	each evening
machen	to do		**viel**	much

Hast du viele Hausaufgaben?	Do you have a lot of homework?
Ich mache jeden Abend eine Stunde Hausaufgaben.	I do homework for an hour every evening.
Gewöhnlich mache ich meine Hausaufgaben von fünf bis sieben Uhr.	I normally do my homework from five to seven o'clock.
Ich muß auch für die Prüfung lernen.	I also have to learn for the exam.

Sieh dir diesen Stundenplan an und beantworte die Fragen.

1. Wie viele Stunden gibt es an einem Tag?
2. Was ist am Dienstag die dritte Stunde?
3. Wann ist die Schule aus?

	Montag	Dienstag
7.30	Geschichte	Deutsch
8.20	Englisch	Deutsch
PAUSE		
9.20	Kunst	Französisch
10.10	Kunst	Sport
GROßE PAUSE		
11.20	Mathe	Musik
12.50	Erdkunde	Mathe

◀ *Home life* ▶

Jobs around the home

abspülen	to wash up	der Babysitter (-)	babysitter (male)
abtrocknen	to dry up	die Babysitterin	babysitter (female)
aufräumen	to tidy	(-nen)	
helfen	to help	der Garten (⁻)	garden
kochen	to cook	das Zimmer (-)	room
den Tisch decken	to set the table	immer	always
waschen	to wash	letztes Wochenende	last weekend
das Bett (-en)	bed	morgen	tomorrow
die Eltern	parents	selbst	oneself

Wie hilfst du bei der Hausarbeit?	What do you do to help at home?
Ich trockne ab.	I dry the dishes.
Ich räume immer mein Zimmer auf.	I always tidy my room.
Nächstes Wochenende werde ich meinen Eltern im Garten helfen.	Next weekend I will help my parents in the garden.
Letztes Wochenende habe ich für meine Eltern das Auto gewaschen.	Last weekend I washed the car for my parents.
Ich mache das selbst.	I do that myself.

Your address and where you live

die Adresse (-n)	address	wohnen	to live
die Straße (-n)	road, street		

Wo wohnst du?	Where do you live?
Ich wohne in ...	I live in ...
Meine Adresse ist ... Straße siebenundzwanzig.	My address is 27 ... Road.

Where you live

der Bungalow (-s)	bungalow	das Hochhaus (⁻er)	high-rise building
das Doppel-haus (⁻er)	semi-detached house	das Reihen-haus (⁻er)	terraced house
das Einzel-haus (⁻er)	detached house	die Wohnung (-en)	flat
das Haus (⁻er)	house	klein	small
		groß	big

Wohnst du in einem Haus oder in einer Wohnung?	Do you live in a house or a flat?
Wir wohnen in einem kleinen, alten Reihenhaus.	We live in a small, old, terraced house.
Ich wohne in einem modernen Doppelhaus.	I live in a modern semi-detached house.
Mein Haus gefällt mir sehr, weil es einen großen Garten hat.	I like my house very much because it has a large garden.

Describe your home and its location

das Dorf (¨er)	village	das Schlaf-	bedroom
die Garage (-n)	garage	zimmer (-)	
das Gebäude (-)	building	die Stadt (¨e)	town
die Stadtmitte (-n)	centre	auf dem Lande	in the country

Wie ist dein Haus?	What is your house like?
Es ist ziemlich groß.	It's quite large.
Es hat zwei Schlafzimmer.	It has two bedrooms.
Wir haben einen Garten und keine Garage.	We've got a garden and no garage.
Wo ist das Haus?	Where is the house?
Es ist in der Stadtmitte.	It's in the town centre.
Ich wohne in einem Dorf.	I live in a village.
Ich wohne auf dem Lande.	I live in the country.

Your home: the rooms, garage and garden; their location, colour, size and contents

das Badezimmer (-)	bathroom	der Sessel (-)	armchair
der Eingang (¨e)	entrance	das Sofa (-s)	sofa
das Eßzimmer (-)	dining room	der Stuhl (¨e)	chair
der Keller (-)	cellar	der Tisch (-e)	table
die Küche (-n)	kitchen	die Treppe (-n)	stairs
das Schlaf-	bedroom	die Tür (-en)	door
zimmer (-)		der Geschirrspül-	dishwasher
die Toilette (-n)	toilet	automat (-en)	
das Wohn-	lounge; living room	die Spül-	dishwasher
zimmer (-)		maschine (-n)	
der Baum (¨e)	tree	der Herd (-e)	oven
die Blume (-n)	flower	der Kühl-	fridge
das Bett (-en)	bed	schrank (¨e)	
das Fenster (-)	window	der Vorhang (¨e)	curtain
der Kleider-	wardrobe	die Wand (¨e)	wall
schrank (¨e)		die Wasch-	washing
die Lampe (-n)	lamp	maschine (-n)	machine
der Schrank (¨e)	cupboard	die Zentralheizung	central heating
der Schreibtisch (-e)	desk	beschreiben	to describe

Kannst du dein Haus beschreiben?	Can you describe your house?
Es gibt ein Eßzimmer, eine Küche und ein Wohnzimmer.	There is a dining room, a kitchen and a lounge.
Die Waschmaschine und der Geschirrspülautomat sind in der Küche.	The washing machine and the dishwasher are in the kitchen.
In meinem Zimmer gibt es ein Bett, einen Kleiderschrank und einen Fernseher.	In my room there is a bed, a wardrobe and a television.

Taking a bath or shower

die Dusche (-n)	shower		**nehmen**	to take
baden	to have a bath		**natürlich**	of course
duschen	to take a shower		**sicher**	certainly; of course

Darf ich duschen?	May I take a shower?
Die Dusche ist neben der Toilette.	The shower is next to the toilet.
Ja, natürlich.	Yes, of course.

Needing soap, toothpaste or a towel

der Föhn (-e)	hairdryer		**brauchen**	to need
das Handtuch (¨er)	towel		**geben**	to give
die Seife	soap		**etwas**	anything; something
die Zahnpasta	toothpaste			

Hast du alles, was du brauchst?	Have you got everything you need?
Brauchst du etwas?	Do you need anything?
Ich habe keinen Föhn.	I haven't got a hairdryer.
Ich habe meine Zahnpasta vergessen.	I've forgotten my toothpaste.
Im Badezimmer ist ein Handtuch.	You'll find a towel in the bathroom.

Lies diese Anzeige. Was hat diese Wohnung? Schreib die Buchstaben von den richtigen Bildern.

Schöne Ferienwohnung
bis zu 6 Personen.
Wohnzimmer, 3 Schlafzimmer,
Küche, Bad/Dusche,
Garten, Terrasse.

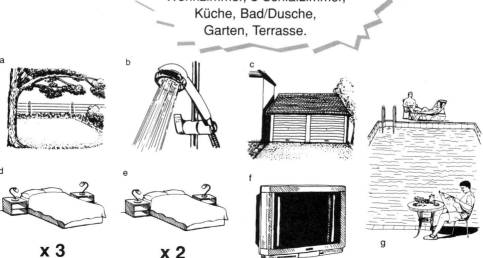

a   b   c

d   e   f

x 3   **x 2**   g

Ask where rooms are

gegenüber	opposite		**neben**	next to
links	on the left		**rechts**	on the right

Wo ist das Badezimmer?	Where is the bathroom?
Es ist hier gegenüber von meinem Schlafzimmer.	It's here opposite my bedroom.
Es ist hier links.	It's here on the left.

Information about mealtimes

das Abendessen	evening meal		**das Mittagessen**	lunch
das Frühstück	breakfast		**gegen**	at about

Wann essen wir?	When do we eat?
Das Abendessen ist um neunzehn Uhr.	Dinner is at seven o'clock.
Wir frühstücken gegen halb neun.	We eat breakfast at about half past eight.

◀ *Media* ▶

Information about TV programmes, radio, music and performers

im Fernsehen	on television		**die Schauspielerin (-nen)**	actress
der Krimi (-s)	crime thriller		**heute abend**	this evening
die Nachrichten	the news		**klasse**	super
das Radio (-s)	radio			
der Schauspieler (-)	actor			

Was gibt es heute abend im Fernsehen?	What's on television this evening?
Es gibt einen guten Krimi.	There's a good thriller.
Der Schauspieler war klasse.	The actor was excellent.
Hast du die Nachrichten im Radio gehört?	Did you hear the news on the radio?

Ask permission to use the telephone, the radio, or watch television

die Eltern	parents		**Darf ich fernsehen?**	May I watch television?
der Fernseher (-)	television		**Könnte ich, bitte, meine Eltern anrufen?**	May I phone my parents please?
das Telefon	telephone			
anrufen	to phone			

Programmes or films you have recently seen and music you have heard

der Film (-e)	film		**das Kino (-s)**	cinema
die Gruppe (-n)	group		**das Programm (-e)**	programme

Warst du im Kino?	Have you been to the cinema?
Gestern war ich im Kino.	I went to the cinema yesterday.
Ich habe einen sehr guten Film gesehen.	I saw a very good film.

Opinions about newspapers, magazines, TV programmes, radio, music and performers

die Presse	the press	**die Zeitung (-en)**	newspaper
der Sänger (-)	singer (male)	**gestern abend**	yesterday evening
die Sängerin (-nen)	singer (female)	**doof**	stupid
die Unter-	entertainment	**interessant**	interesting
haltung		**komisch**	funny
die Sendung (-en)	programme	**denken (an)**	to think (of)
die Zeitschrift (-en)	magazine	**lachen**	to laugh

Hast du diese Zeitschrift gesehen?	Have you read this magazine?
Ja, sie ist sehr interessant.	Yes, it's very interesting.
Hast du die Sendung gestern abend im Fernsehen gesehen?	Did you see the programme on television last night?
Ich sehe Krimis nicht sehr gern.	I don't like watching thrillers very much.
Der Film gestern abend hat mir gut gefallen.	I liked the film yesterday evening.

Ask if someone agrees

einverstanden	I agree	**meinen**	to think

Was meinst du?	What do you think?
Der Film war gut, nicht?	The film was good, wasn't it?
Hat dir die Gruppe gefallen?	Did you like the group?

◄ *Health and fitness* ►

How you feel

der Durst (nach)	thirst (for)	**kalt**	cold
besser	better	**krank**	ill
durstig	thirsty	**müde**	tired
erkältet	to have a cold	**total**	totally; completely
gesund	healthy	**fühlen (sich)**	to feel
heiß	hot	**Hunger haben**	to be hungry
hungrig	hungry		

Wie geht's?	How are you?
Geht es dir besser?	Do you feel better?
Es geht.	I'm alright.
Es geht mir besser.	I feel better.
Es geht mir nicht gut.	I don't feel well.
Mir ist kalt.	I feel cold.
Mir ist heiß.	I feel hot.
Bist du hungrig?	Are you hungry?
Ich bin durstig.	I am thirsty.

Say where you have pain

Bauchschmerzen/ Bauchweh	tummy ache	Zahnschmerzen	toothache
Durchfall	diarrhoea	Magenschmerzen	stomach ache
Fieber	temperature	der Schnupfen	cold
die Grippe	flu	passieren	to happen
Halsschmerzen	sore throat	weh tun	to hurt

Die Körperteile	**Parts of the body**		
der Arm (-e)	arm	das Gesicht (-er)	face
der Bauch	stomach	die Hand (¨e)	hand
das Bein (-e)	leg	der Hals (¨e)	throat
der Finger (-)	finger	der Kopf (¨e)	head
der Fuß (¨sse)	foot	der Magen	stomach
Zahnschmerzen	toothache	die Nase	nose
Magenschmerzen	stomach ache	das Ohr (-en)	ear
der Schnupfen	cold	der Rücken	back
passieren	to happen	der Zahn (¨e)	tooth
weh tun	to hurt		

Was ist los?	What's wrong?
Was ist passiert?	What happened?
Wo tut es weh?	Where does it hurt?
Tut es dir weh?	Does it hurt?
Mein Bein tut weh.	My leg hurts.
Ich habe Halsschmerzen.	I've got a sore throat.
Ich habe Kopfschmerzen.	I've got a headache.
Ich glaube, ich habe Fieber.	I think I've got a temperature.
Ich habe Grippe.	I've got flu.
Ich habe einen Schnupfen.	I've got a cold.

Call for help

Hilfe!	Help!
Können Sie mir bitte helfen?	Can you help me, please?

Note: For consulting a doctor, dentist or chemist see page 57.

◀ *Food* ▶

Opinions about food

Das Obst	**Fruit**	die Kirsche (-n)	cherry
der Apfel (¨)	apple	die Orange (-n)	orange
die Apfelsine (-n)	orange	der Pfirsich (-e)	peach
die Banane (-n)	banana	die Pflaume (-n)	plum
die Erdbeere (-n)	strawberry	die Zitrone (-n)	lemon
die Himbeere (-n)	raspberry		

Das Gemüse	**Vegetables**	die Pommes	chips
Chips	crisps	die Pommes Frites	chips
die Kartoffel (-n)	potato	die Tomate (-n)	tomato

Die Getränke	Drinks
der Apfelsaft	apple juice
das Bier	beer
die Cola	coca cola
das Getränk (-e)	drink
der Kaffee	coffee
der Kakao	cocoa
die Limo	lemonade
das Mineralwasser	mineral water

die Milch	milk
der Orangensaft	orange juice
der Saft	(fruit) juice
die Schokolade	chocolate
der Tee	tea
der Wein	wine
der Rotwein	red wine
der Weißwein	white wine
das Wasser (-)	water

Das Essen	Food
der Aufschnitt	slices of cold meat
die Bockwurst (¨e)	type of pork sausage
der/das Bonbon (-s)	sweet
die Bratwurst (¨e)	grilled sausage
das Brot	bread
das belegte Brot	sandwich
das Brötchen (-)	bread roll
die Butter	butter
Chips	crisps
die Currywurst (¨e)	sausage in curry sauce
das Ei (-er)	egg
das Eis	ice cream
der Fisch (-e)	fish
der Imbiß (-sse)	snack
das Hähnchen	chicken
der/das Joghurt	yoghurt
der Käse	cheese
der Kaugummi	chewing-gum
der Keks (-e)	biscuit
der Kuchen (-)	cake
der Pfeffer	pepper

die Praline (-n)	chocolate
der Reis	rice
das Rindfleisch	beef
die Sahne	cream
der Salat	salad
das Salz	salt
der Schinken	ham
das Schweinefleisch	pork
der Senf	mustard
das Spiegelei (-er)	fried egg
die Suppe	soup
die Torte (n)	cream cake
die Wurst (¨e)	sausage
das Würstchen (-)	small sausage
der Zucker	sugar

mitnehmen	to take away
probieren	to try (taste)
schmecken	to taste
trinken	to drink
scharf	spicy
süß	sweet

Es schmeckt sehr gut.	It tastes very good.
Ißt du gern Hähnchen?	Do you like chicken?
Ich esse sehr gern Wurst.	I love sausage.
Ich trinke gern Orangensaft.	I like orange juice.
Ich esse nicht gern Currywurst.	I don't like sausage in curry sauce.
Sie ist mir zu scharf.	It's too spicy for me.
Wir essen oft Pommes Frites.	We often eat chips.
Wir trinken gewöhnlich Kaffee.	We usually drink coffee.

Wo kann man die Pizza essen?

Accept and decline offers of food and drink

ein bißchen	a little	**lecker**	delicious
genug	enough		

Möchtest du Pommes?	Would you like some chips?
Möchtest du etwas Erdbeertorte?	Would you like some strawberry tart?
Noch etwas Kaffee?	Some more coffee?
Ja, gerne.	Yes, please.
Nein, danke.	No, thank you.
Das war lecker.	It was delicious.

Ask for food and table items

die Gabel (-n)	fork	**das Messer (-)**	knife
der Löffel (-)	spoon		

Entschuldigen Sie, bitte. Ich habe keine Gabel.	Excuse me, please. I haven't got a fork.
Gib mir das Salz, bitte.	Pass me the salt, please.
Könnten Sie mir den Senf geben, bitte?	Could you pass me the mustard, please?
Ich möchte noch etwas Brot, bitte.	I'd like a little more bread, please.

Call the waiter or waitress

Herr Ober!	To attract the waiter's attention.	**Fräulein!**	To attract the attention of the waitress.

Order a drink or simple meal

das Café (-s)	café	**die Tasse (-n)**	cup
das Glas (¨er)	glass	**beide**	both
das Kännchen (-)	pot	**bestellen**	to order
der Nachtisch	dessert	**bringen**	to bring
die Speisekarte (-n)	menu		

Bitte sehr?	Can I help you?
Die Speisekarte, bitte.	The menu, please.
Einmal Hähnchen.	One chicken.
Und zu trinken?	And to drink?
Ich möchte eine Tasse Kaffee.	I'd like a cup of coffee.
Ich möchte ein Kännchen Kaffee.	I'd like a pot of coffee.
Als Nachtisch hätte ich gern ein Eis.	For dessert, I'd like an ice cream.

Ask about availability

haben	to have	**was für?**	what kind of?

Haben Sie Eis?	Have you got ice cream?
Ist noch etwas Suppe da?	Is there any more soup?
Was für Kuchen haben Sie?	What sort of cakes have you got?

Ask for a fixed price menu

das Menü (-s)	fixed-price menu	**nehmen**	to take

Bitte sehr?	Can I help you?
Ich nehme das Menü, bitte.	I'll have the fixed-price menu, please.
Das Menü zu DM20, bitte.	The DM20 menu, please.

Ask for an explanation

genau	exactly	**warm**	warm
typisch	typical	**wie**	like

Was genau ist Schnitzel?	What is Schnitzel exactly?
Ist es warm oder kalt?	Is it hot or cold?
Es ist wie eine Wurst.	It's like a sausage.
Es ist typisch deutsch.	It's typically German.

Opinions about a meal

schrecklich	awful	**wirklich**	really

Das war wirklich lecker.	That was really delicious.
Der Käse war besonders gut.	The cheese was particularly good.
Die Pommes Frites waren kalt.	The chips were cold.
Es war schrecklich.	It was awful.

Ask where the toilet or telephone is

das Telefon	telephone	**unten**	downstairs
die Toilette (-n)	toilet	**wo?**	where?

Entschuldigen Sie, wo sind hier die Toiletten?	Excuse me, where are the toilets here?
Das Telefon ist unten neben den Toiletten.	The telephone is downstairs next to the toilets.
Gibt es ein Telefon?	Is there a telephone?

Ask for the bill

die Rechnung (-en)	bill	**zahlen**	to pay
einzeln	separately		

Zahlen, bitte.	The bill, please.
Was macht das, bitte?	What does that come to, please?
Stimmt es?	Is it correct?
Es tut mir leid.	I'm sorry.

Lies die Speisekarte und beantworte die Fragen unten.

1. Gerd ißt nicht gern Kartoffeln. Was soll er als Hauptgang bestellen?
2. Uschi ißt nicht gern Obst. Was soll sie als Nachtisch bestellen?
3. Herr Meyer trinkt keinen Alkohol. Was soll er als Getränk bestellen?

Die Speisekarte

Hauptgang

Hähnchen mit Pommes

Wurst m. Kartoffelsalat

Schinkenomelett mit Salat

Nachtisch

Erdbeertorte

Apfelkuchen

Schokoeis

Getränke

Apfelsaft

Bier

Weißwein

PERSONAL AND SOCIAL LIFE

◀ *Self, family and friends* ▶

Information about self, family, friends and pets

Die Leute	**People**	**der Junge (-n)**	boy
das Baby (-s)	baby	**das Kind (-er)**	child
der/die Bekannte	acquaintance	**das Mädchen (-)**	girl
der Bruder (⸚)	brother	**der Mann (⸚er)**	man
die Dame (-n)	lady	**der Mensch (-en)**	person
das Einzelkind (-er)	only child	**die Mutter (⸚)**	mother
die Eltern	parents	**Mutti**	mum
der Engländer (-)	Englishman	**der Nachbar (-n)**	neighbour
die Engländerin (-nen)	English woman	**die Oma**	grandmother
		Omi	grandma
der Erwachsene (-n)	adult	**der Onkel (-)**	uncle
die Familie (-n)	family	**der Opa**	grandfather
die Frau (-en)	woman; Mrs.	**Opi**	grandad
der Freund (-e)	friend	**die Schwester (-n)**	sister
die Freundin (-nen)	friend	**der Sohn (⸚e)**	son
die Geschwister	brothers and sisters	**die Tante (-n)**	aunt
die Großeltern	grandparents	**die Tochter (⸚)**	daughter
die Großmutter (⸚)	grandmother	**der Vater (⸚)**	father
der Großvater (⸚)	grandfather	**Vati**	dad
der Herr (-en)	man; Mr.	**der Zwilling (-e)**	twin
Die Haustiere	**Pets**	**das Meerschweinchen (-)**	guinea pig
der Goldfisch (-e)	goldfish	**das Pferd (-e)**	horse
die Maus (⸚e)	mouse	**das Tier (-e)**	animal
der Hund (-e)	dog	**der Vogel (⸚)**	bird
das Kaninchen (-)	rabbit	**der Wellensittich (-e)**	budgerigar
die Katze (-n)	cat		

Words to describe people and pets

das Auge (-n)	eye	**intelligent**	intelligent
der Bart	beard	**jung**	young
die Brille	glasses	**lustig**	cheerful
das Haar	hair	**reich**	rich
der Schnurrbart	moustache	**schlank**	slender
allein	alone	**schmal**	slim, slender
arm	poor	**schön**	lovely, beautiful
blond	blonde	**schwach**	weak
böse	angry	**stark**	strong
dick	fat	**manchmal**	sometimes
dumm	stupid	**oft**	often
dünn	thin	**aussehen**	to look like
faul	lazy	**das Alter**	age
fleißig	hard-working	**das Datum (Daten)**	date
freundlich	friendly	**die Geburt (-en)**	birth
glücklich	happy	**der Geburtstag (-e)**	birthday
häßlich	ugly	**feiern**	to celebrate
hübsch	pretty	**geboren**	born

Sag mir etwas über deine Eltern.	Tell me something about your parents.
Hast du Geschwister?	Have you got any brothers or sisters?
Ich habe einen Bruder und zwei Schwestern.	I've got a brother and two sisters.
Ich bin ein Einzelkind.	I'm an only child.
Hast du Haustiere?	Have you got any pets?
Ich habe eine Katze.	I've got a cat.
Sie heißt Mitzi.	She's called Mitzi.
Er ist sieben.	He's seven.
Sie hat am vierundzwanzigsten Mai Geburtstag.	Her birthday is on the 24th of May.
Sie ist Engländerin.	She is English.
Sie liest gern.	She likes reading.
Sie ist manchmal fleißig und auch glücklich.	She is sometimes hard-working and also happy.
Er hat blonde Haare.	He's got blonde hair.
Er hat braune Augen.	He's got brown eyes.

Welches Bild paßt zu diesem Text?

Ich bin sechzehn Jahre alt. Ich habe einen Bruder, er ist acht, und eine Schwester, die erst zwei Jahre alt ist. Ich habe auch ein Meerschweinchen und ein Kaninchen.

Spell your name, street and town

Deutschland	Germany	**die Staatsangehörig-**	nationality
England	England	**keit**	
das Land (ᐟer)	country	**die Unterschrift**	signature
der Name (-n)	name	**der Vorname (-n)**	first name
die Postleit-	post code	**der Wohnort**	place of residence
zahl (-en)		**unterschreiben**	to sign

Wie heißt du?	What are you called?
Wie schreibt man das?	How do you write that?
Wie ist deine Postleitzahl?	What's your post code?
Wie heißt deine Stadt?	What is your town called?

◀ *Free time, holidays and special occasions* ▶

Hobbies and interests

angeln	to fish	**wandern**	to hike; to walk for
ausgehen	to go out		pleasure
Badminton spielen	to play badminton	**der Computer**	computer
fotografieren	to take photos	**die Freizeit**	free time
Fußball spielen	to play football	**das Foto**	photo
kegeln	to play skittles	**der Fotoapparat**	camera
Musik hören	to listen to music	**das Hallenbad (ᐟer)**	swimming baths
radfahren	to cycle	**das Hobby (s)**	hobby
reiten	to ride	**das Instrument (e)**	musical instrument
Rollschuh fahren	to roller skate	**das Interesse (n)**	interest
sammeln	to collect	**der Jugendklub**	youth club
schwimmen	to swim	**Tennis**	tennis
singen	to sing	**Tischtennis**	table tennis
skifahren	to ski	**manchmal**	sometimes
spazierengehen	to go for a walk	**besichtigen**	to visit (something)
Sport treiben	to do sport	**programmieren**	to program (a
tanzen	to dance		computer)
		die Stereoanlage (n)	stereo system

Was machst du in deiner Freizeit?	What do you do in your free time?
Ich gehe jedes Wochenende schwimmen.	I go swimming every weekend.
Letzten Samstag habe ich Fußball gespielt.	Last Saturday I played football.
Gestern bin ich angeln gegangen.	I went fishing yesterday.
Manchmal gehe ich in die Stadt.	I go into town sometimes.
Übermorgen gehe ich zum Jugendklub.	I'm going to the youth club the day after tomorrow.

What are you not allowed to do here?

Radfahren und Reiten verboten!

Express simple opinions

die Band	the band		freuen	to be pleased
die Mann-schaft (-en)	team		sich freuen auf	to look forward to
			gewinnen	to win
das Spiel	the game		laufen	to run
das Theater-stück (-e)	the play (at a theatre)		gerade	just

Ich fahre sehr gern Ski.	I like skiing very much.
Ich spiele lieber Tennis.	I prefer playing tennis.
Warum?	Why?
Es ist gesund.	It's good for you.
Wir haben heute gut gespielt.	We played well today.
Gestern haben wir gewonnen.	We won yesterday.
Wir freuen uns auf das Theaterstück.	We are looking forward to the play.
Das freut mich.	I'm pleased.
Ich spiele am liebsten Fußball.	I like playing football most of all.
Das macht Spaß.	It's fun.
Ich habe gerade Tischtennis gespielt.	I've just played table tennis.

Agree or disagree with opinions

die Idee (-n)	idea

Das finde ich auch.	I think so too.
Das meine ich auch.	I agree.
Tanzt du gern?	Do you like dancing?
Nein, ich treibe nicht gern Sport.	No, I don't like doing sport.
Ich auch nicht.	Neither do I.
In Ordnung.	Agreed; alright.

Describe a recent holiday or leisure activity

der Ausflug (-̈e)	excursion		die See	sea
der Besuch (-e)	the visit		(zu) Ostern	(at) Easter
die Discothek (-en)	discotheque		die Rundfahrt (-en)	tour
die Fahrt (-en)	the journey		die Woche (-n)	week
die Ferien	holidays		abends	in the evenings
das Flugzeug (-e)	plane		bei	at the house of
das Meer (-e)	sea		vorgestern	the day before yesterday
der See (-n)	lake			

Was hast du in den Ferien gemacht?	What did you do in the holidays?
Ich war in Deutschland.	I went to Germany.
Ich war bei meinen Großeltern.	I stayed with my grandparents.
Wir waren zwei Wochen dort.	We were there for two weeks.
Wir haben viele Ausflüge gemacht.	We went on lots of excursions.
Wir sind oft schwimmen gegangen.	We often went swimming.
Zu Ostern waren wir in Schottland.	We went to Scotland at Easter.
Abends sind wir in die Discothek gegangen.	We went to the discotheque in the evenings.

Mit wem warst du weg?	Who did you go with?
Mit meinen Eltern.	With my parents.

Die Monate	The months	**August,**	August,
Der Wievielte ist es?	What's the date?	**September,**	September,
Januar, Februar,	January, February,	**Oktober, November,**	October, November,
März, April,	March, April,	**Dezember.**	December.
Mai, Juni, Juli,	May, June, July,		

Im Februar bin ich zu Hause geblieben.	I stayed at home in February.

Einige Länder	Some countries		
Belgien	Belgium	**Irland**	Ireland
Deutschland	Germany	**Italien**	Italy
Frankreich	France	**Österreich**	Austria
Griechenland	Greece	**die Schweiz**	Switzerland
Großbritannien	Great Britain	**Spanien**	Spain
Holland	Holland	**die Türkei**	Turkey

Die Wochentage	The days	**Donnerstag**	Thursday
Sonntag	Sunday	**Freitag**	Friday
Montag	Monday	**Samstag**	Saturday
Dienstag	Tuesday	**Sonnabend**	Saturday (you can use either word)
Mittwoch	Wednesday		

Preferences and alternatives for going out

die Discothek (-en)	discotheque	**das Konzert (-e)**	concert
der Fan	fan	**das Theater (-)**	theatre
das Fitnesszentrum (-zentren)	keep fit centre	**der Zoo (-s)**	zoo
das Museum (Museen)	museum	**ich möchte lieber**	I'd prefer
		treffen	to meet
das Sportzentrum (-zentren)	sports centre	**jetzt**	now
		lieber	rather
		vielleicht	perhaps

Was willst du machen?	What do you want to do?
Ich möchte lieber ins Kino gehen.	I'd prefer to go to the cinema.
Was läuft?	What's on?
Möchtest du jetzt in die Stadt gehen?	Would you like to go to town now?
Möchtest du lieber zum Sportzentrum gehen?	Would you prefer to go to the sports centre?
Gehen wir vielleicht in die Disco?	Shall we perhaps go to the disco?

Times and prices at leisure facilities

der Eintritt	entry; admission	**das Schwimm- bad (¨er)**	swimming baths
das Endspiel (-e)	final (match)	**der Sportplatz (¨e)**	sports ground
das Freibad (¨er)	outdoor swimming pool	**das Stadion (Stadien)**	stadium
der Preis	price	**die Vorstellung (-en)**	performance
		anfangen	to begin

Wann fängt das Spiel an?	When does the match begin?
Der Film endet um zweiundzwanzig Uhr.	The film ends at ten o'clock.
Wo ist das Spiel Samstag?	Where is the match on Saturday?
Wann ist das Hallenbad auf?	When are the swimming baths open?

Buy tickets for leisure facilities

das Boot (-e)	boat		**die Kasse**	cash desk
die Karte (-n)	ticket		**kosten**	to cost

Was kostet eine Karte, bitte?	What does a ticket cost, please?
Zweimal, bitte.	Two tickets, please.

Pocket money

die CD (-s)	CD		**kaufen**	to buy
das Geld	money		**sparen**	to save
die Kassette (-n)	cassette		**bekommen**	to get
die Schallplatte (-n)	record		**verdienen**	to earn
das Taschengeld	pocket money		**genug**	enough
der Walkman	walkman			

Wieviel Taschengeld bekommst du?	How much pocket money do you get?
Ich bekomme drei Pfund pro Woche.	I get £3 a week.
Ist das genug?	Is that enough?
Ich arbeite auch in einem Geschäft, um Geld zu verdienen.	I also work in a shop to earn money.
Was machst du mit dem Geld?	What do you do with the money?
Ich kaufe CDs.	I buy CDs.
Ich spare mein Geld.	I save my money.

◄ *Personal relationships & social activities* ►

Greet people

Grüß Gott!	Hello! (in Bavaria)		**Vielen Dank.**	Thank you very much.
Willkommen in England!	Welcome to England!		**Auf Wiedersehen.**	Goodbye
Guten Tag.	Hello		**Tschüß.**	Goodbye (you use this to say goodbye to friends)
Guten Morgen.	Good morning			
Guten Abend.	Good evening			
Gute Nacht.	Good night		**Hallo.**	Hello (on phone)
Servus!	Hello (to a friend)		**Auf Wiederhören.**	Goodbye (on phone)

Ask how people are

Grüß dich! Wie geht's?	Hello! How are you? (to a friend)		**Und Ihnen?**	And you? (if you are talking to an adult)
Und dir?	And you? (if you are talking to a friend)			

Make informal introductions

Darf ich meine Mutter vorstellen?	May I introduce my mother?	**die Brieffreundin (-nen)**	penfriend
der Brieffreund (-e)	penfriend	**Das ist mein Bruder.**	This is my brother.

Invite someone to come in and sit down

hereinkommen to come in   **sich setzen** to sit down

Komm rein.	Come in (to a friend).
Setz dich.	Sit down (to a friend).
Kommen Sie rein.	Come in (to an adult).
Setzen Sie sich, bitte.	Please sit down (to an adult).

Welcome a visitor

hoffen to hope   **hoffentlich** I hope that   **die Reise (-n)** journey   **wieder** again

Hoffentlich hast du eine gute Reise gehabt.	I hope you've had a good journey.
Möchtest du etwas essen?	Would you like something to eat?
Was möchtest du machen?	What would you like to do?
Hier ist dein Schlafzimmer.	This is your bedroom.

Thank for hospitality

die Gastfreundschaft hospitality   **bald** soon   **danke** thank you   **danken** to thank   **nie** never

Vielen Dank für Ihre Gastfreundschaft.	Thank you very much for your hospitality.
Es war sehr schön.	It was lovely.
Ich werde meinen Urlaub hier nie vergessen.	I'll never forget the holidays (I spent) here.
Hoffentlich kommst du bald zu uns.	I hope you'll soon come to see us.

◄ *Arranging a meeting or activity* ►

Suggestions for going out

einladen to invite   **warten (auf)** to wait (for)   **heute nachmittag** this afternoon   **nachher** afterwards   **sogar** even

Möchtest du heute abend zu mir kommen?	Would you like to come to my house this evening?
Gehen wir morgen ins Konzert?	Shall we go to a concert tomorrow?
Was machst du heute abend?	What are you doing this evening?

Wir können sogar ins Hallenbad gehen.	We could even go to the swimming baths.
Ich gehe heute abend ins Theater.	I'm going to the theatre this evening.
Kommst du mit?	Are you coming with me?
Ich möchte Sie heute abend in ein Restaurant einladen.	I'd like to invite you to go to a restaurant this evening.
Wir spielen danach Tennis.	We're playing tennis afterwards.
Möchtest du mitspielen?	Do you want to play with us?

Wann und wo trifft Klaus seine Freunde?

Accept or decline an invitation

die Einladung (-en)	invitation	sich entschuldigen	to apologise
bleiben	to stay	vielen Dank	thank you very much
Entschuldigung	sorry	zu Hause	at home
nett	nice; kind	es tut mir leid	I am sorry
spät	late		

Vielen Dank für die Einladung.	Thank you very much for the invitation.
Es tut mir leid, ich kann nicht ins Kino kommen.	Sorry I can't come to the cinema.
Das war sehr nett von Ihnen, aber ich muß zu Hause bleiben.	That was very kind of you, but I must stay at home.
Ich möchte gerne zu dir kommen.	I'd very much like to come to your house.
Das ist mir egal.	I don't mind.

Express pleasure

froh	glad		**nett**	nice, kind
gut	good		**toll**	great, super

Das ist aber nett!	That's really nice!
Gute Idee!	Good idea!
Ich möchte gerne mitkommen.	I'd really like to come.

Arrange a time and place to meet

die Bushalte-	bus stop		**stehen**	to stand
stelle (-n)			**treffen**	to meet

Wann sollen wir uns treffen?	When should we meet?
Um elf Uhr?	At eleven o'clock?
Wo treffen wir uns?	Where shall we meet?
An der Bushaltestelle.	At the bus stop.
Bei mir.	At my house.

◀ *Leisure and entertainment* ▶

Ask the cost of seats and buy tickets, ask what is on at the cinema

die Ermäßigung	reduction		**der Sonderpreis**	special price

Was läuft?	What's on?
Ein Krimi.	A thriller.
Was für ein Film ist es?	What sort of film is it?
Gibt es einen Sonderpreis für Studenten?	Is there a special price for students?
Zweimal, bitte.	Two tickets, please.
Gibt es eine Ermäßigung für Studenten?	Is there a reduction for students?

Starting and finishing times

eine Sekunde (-n)	second		**die Vorstel-**	performance
die Uhrzeit	time of day		**lung (-en)**	

Wann beginnt die letzte Vorstellung?	When does the last performance begin?
Um neunzehn Uhr dreißig.	At 7.30pm.

Opinions about events

furchtbar	dreadful		**finden**	to find
mies	rubbish		**also**	so; therefore
schrecklich	terrible		**ganz**	quite
spitze	great		**noch nicht**	not yet

Es war wirklich klasse.	It was really great.
Hat dir der Film gefallen?	Did you like the film?
Ich habe den Film noch nicht gesehen.	I haven't seen the film yet.
War es ein gutes Spiel?	Was it a good match?
Es war gar nicht mal schlecht.	It wasn't at all bad.
Ich finde, es war ein ganz guter Film.	I think it was quite a good film.

? Wann beginnt die letzte Vorstellung von diesem Film?

KINO CENTER

Samstag, 30 Juli
17.00 u. 18.30 Uhr

101 DALMATINER

Hier wird Kino zum Vergnügen!

WALT DISNEY'S Zeichentrickspaß für die ganze Familie.

South East Essex College
of Arts & Technology
Carnarvon Road Southend-on-Sea Essex SS2 6LS
Tel: (01702) 220400 Fax: (01702) 432320 Minicom: (01702) 220642

THE WORLD AROUND US

◀ *Home town, local environment and customs* ▶

Your home town and region

der Berg (-e)	mountain	der Tourist (-en)	tourist (male)
die Brücke (-n)	bridge	die Touristin (-nen)	tourist (female)
der Einwohner (-)	inhabitant	herrlich	lovely
die Gegend (-en)	area, region	hoch	high
die Industrie (-n)	industry	mittelgroß	medium-sized
die Landschaft (-en)	scenery	sauber	clean
der Ort (-e)	place	schmutzig	dirty
das Rathaus (¨er)	town hall	wenig	little; few

Ist es eine schöne Stadt?	Is it an attractive town?
Es ist eine mittelgroße Stadt.	It's a medium-sized town.
Es gibt viel Industrie.	There's a lot of industry.
Die Gegend ist herrlich.	The area is lovely.
Was gibt es zu sehen?	What is there to see?
Es gibt schöne, hohe Berge.	There are lovely, high mountains.
Ich mag die Stadt nicht, weil es so viele Touristen gibt.	I don't like the town because there are so many tourists.

Show a visitor around your town

die Aussicht	view	die Sehens-	sight, something
der Dom (-e)	cathedral	würdigkeit (-en)	worth seeing
der Fluß (¨sse)	river	der Verkehr	traffic
das Gebäude (-)	building	dort	there
die Kirche (-n)	church	am Ende	at the end
der Marktplatz (¨e)	marketplace	sehen	to see
der Park (-s)	park	zeigen	to show
das Schloß (¨sser)	castle		

Möchtest du in die Stadt gehen?	Would you like to go to town?
Es gibt viel zu sehen.	There's lots to see.
Hier ist der Marktplatz.	Here's the market place.
Dort rechts ist der alte Dom.	There on the right is the old cathedral.
Am Ende dieser Straße sehen Sie das Schloß.	At the end of this street you'll see the castle.
Sie gehen an der Kirche vorbei.	You go past the church.

Going into town

die Straßenbahn	tram	ungefähr	approximately

Wie kommst du in die Stadt?	How do you get to town?
Es gibt eine Bushaltestelle neben unserem Haus.	There's a bus stop next to our house.

Ich fahre gewöhnlich mit der Straßenbahn.	I usually go by tram.
Wie oft fährt eine Straßenbahn?	How often is there a tram?
Alle zwanzig Minuten.	Every twenty minutes.
Wie lange dauert die Reise?	How long does the journey take?
Ungefähr zehn Minuten.	About ten minutes.

Important festivals

das Fest	festival	Silvesterabend	New Year's Eve
Fasching	carnival celebrated in February in Germany	Weihnachten	Christmas
		der erste Januar	January 1st
		der fünfundzwan-	December 25th
Heiligabend	Christmas Eve	zigste Dezember	
Karneval	Carnival	das Geschenk	present
Neujahr	New Year's Day	die Karte	card
Ostern	Easter	stattfinden	to take place

Ich finde Ostern so schön.	I like Easter so much.
Am Heiligabend gehen wir in die Kirche.	We go to church on Christmas eve.
Ich schicke viele Weihnachtskarten.	I send lots of Christmas cards.
Wir bekommen Geschenke.	We get presents.
Zu Ostern machen wir bunte Eier.	At Easter we make brightly-coloured eggs.

Understand weather forecasts

der Blitz	lightning	der Sturm (ˉe)	storm
der Donner	thunder	der Wind	wind
der Frost	frost	der Grad	degree
das Gewitter	storm	der Vormittag	morning
der Nebel	fog	das Wetter	weather
der Regen	rain	die Wetter-	weather forecast
der Schauer	shower	vorhersage	
der Schnee	snow	es blitzt	there's lightning
die Sonne	sun	es donnert	there's thunder
frieren	to freeze	schön	nice; lovely
regnen	to rain	stürmisch	stormy
scheinen	to shine	trocken	dry
schneien	to snow	warm	warm
kühl	cool	wahrscheinlich	probably
naß	wet	windig	windy
neblig	foggy	wolkig	cloudy
sonnig	sunny		

Wie wird das Wetter morgen?	What will the weather be like tomorrow?
Es soll schneien.	It's supposed to snow.
Am Vormittag wird es kühl sein.	It will be cool in the morning.
In der Nacht wird es wahrscheinlich frieren.	It will probably freeze in the night.
Am Nachmittag wird es wolkig sein.	It will be cloudy in the afternoon.

Understand and describe weather conditions

Die Jahreszeiten	The seasons	**fast**	almost
der Frühling	Spring	**heiß**	hot
der Sommer	Summer	**immer**	always
der Herbst	Autumn	**oft**	often
der Winter	Winter	**plötzlich**	suddenly

Im Winter ist es gewöhnlich kalt.	It's usually cold in winter.
Im Herbst ist es oft neblig.	It's often foggy in the autumn.
Sieh mal, es schneit!	Look, it's snowing!
Bei so heißem Wetter kommt oft ein Gewitter.	Such hot weather often brings a storm.
In dieser Gegend regnet es viel.	It rains a lot in this area.
Es hat gestern stark geregnet.	It rained heavily yesterday.
Es war immer sonnig.	It was always sunny.

◀ *Finding the way* ▶

Attract the attention of a passer-by

Entschuldigen Sie, bitte.	Excuse me please.	**Entschuldigung.**	Excuse me.

Ask and state where a place is

die Autobahn (-en)	motorway	**der Parkplatz (¨e)**	car park
der Bahnhof (¨e)	station	**die Polizeiwache**	police station
die Haltestelle (-n)	stop	**die Post**	post office
der Flughafen	airport	**die Tankstelle (-n)**	petrol station
die Innenstadt	town centre	**die U-Bahn**	underground
das Krankenhaus (¨er)	hospital	**das Verkehrsamt**	tourist information office
die Kreuzung	crossroads		

Ask how to get to a place

an	on	**vor**	in front of
auf	on	**von**	from
aus	out of	**zu**	to
bis	up to; as far as	**zwischen**	between
dann	then	**dort drüben**	over there
durch	through	**entlang**	along
gegenüber	opposite	**erst**	first
hinter	behind	**geradeaus**	straight on
in	in	**nächste**	next
nach	to; after	**es gibt**	there is; there are
über	over	**der Stadtplan (¨e)**	street map
unter	under	**nehmen**	to take

Wo ist hier eine Tankstelle?	Where is there a petrol station here?
Es gibt einen Parkplatz am Markt.	There's a car park at the market.
Sie gehen hier rechts.	You go right here.
Sie nehmen die erste Straße links.	You take the first street on the left.
Sie gehen bis zur Kirche.	You go as far as the church.
Die Post ist gegenüber vom Bahnhof.	The post office is opposite the station.
Sie gehen an der Post vorbei.	You go past the post office.
Wie komme ich zum Schloß, bitte?	How do I get to the castle, please?
Wie komme ich zur nächsten Post, bitte?	How do I get to the nearest post office, please?
Wie komme ich zur Stadtmitte?	How do I get to the town centre?

Nearby or far away?

der Kilometer (-)	kilometre		nur	only
die Meile (-n)	mile		in der Nähe	nearby
die Minute	minute		weit	far
die Richtung	direction		ziemlich	quite
am besten	best			

Das ist nur fünf Minuten von hier.	That is only five minutes from here.
Das ist hier in der Nähe.	It is nearby.
Ist es weit?	Is it far?
Ja, es ist ziemlich weit.	Yes, it is quite a long way.
Am besten fahren Sie mit dem Bus.	It's best to take the bus.
Es ist ganz in der Nähe.	It's just near here.
In Richtung Hamburg.	In the direction of Hamburg.

Express thanks

Danke schön.	Thank you very much.	Bitte schön.	Don't mention it.

Was kann man in Interspar machen?

◀ *Shopping* ▶

Finding shops and supermarkets

die Apotheke (-n)	chemist where you can change a prescription	**das Geschäft (-e)**	shop
		das Kaufhaus (-̈er)	department store
		die Konditorei (-en)	cake shop
die Bäckerei (-en)	baker's	**das Lebensmittel-**	grocer's shop
das Buchgeschäft (-e)	bookshop	**geschäft (-e)**	
die Drogerie (-n)	chemist which does not sell medicines on prescription	**die Metzgerei (-en)**	butcher's
		der Supermarkt (-̈e)	supermarket
		einkaufen	to go shopping

Wo ist die Bäckerei?	Where is the baker's?
Gibt es eine Metzgerei hier in der Nähe?	Is there a butcher's near here?
Wo gibt es einen Supermarkt?	Where is there a supermarket?
Wo ist die nächste Apotheke?	Where is the nearest chemist's?
Wo kann ich Brot kaufen?	Where can I buy some bread?

? Was für ein Geschäft ist das?

Colour, size, who an item is for

Die Kleidung	**Clothes**	**der Pulli (-s)**	pullover
der Badeanzug (-̈e)	swimsuit	**der Pullover (-)**	pullover
die Badehose (-n)	swimming trunks	**der Rock (-̈e)**	skirt
die Bluse (-n)	blouse	**die Sandale (-n)**	sandal
der Handschuh (-e)	glove	**der Schlaf-**	pyjamas
das Hemd (-en)	shirt	**anzug (-̈e)**	
die Hose (-n)	trousers	**der Schmuck**	jewellery
die Jacke (-n)	jacket	**der Schuh (-e)**	shoe
Jeans	jeans	**die Socke (-n)**	sock
das Kleid (-er)	dress	**die Sonnen-**	sunglasses
die Kleidung	clothes	**brille (-n)**	
die Krawatte (-n)	tie	**der Strumpf (-̈e)**	sock
der Mantel (-̈)	coat	**die Strumpfhose (-n)**	tights
die Mütze (-n)	cap	**das T-Shirt (-s)**	T-shirt

Die Farben	Colours
blau	blue
braun	brown
bunt	brightly coloured
dunkel	dark
gelb	yellow
grau	grey
grün	green
hell	light
lila	mauve
orange	orange
rosa	pink
rot	red
schwarz	black

türkis	turquoise
weiß	white
die Größe	size
aus Leder	made of leather
aus Baumwolle	made of cotton
mittelgroß	medium-sized
anprobieren	to try on
anhaben	to have on
ausziehen	to take off
die Mode (-n)	fashion
die Sonnencreme (-s)	sun cream
das Souvenir (-s)	souvenir

Ich möchte einen Pulli aus Wolle.	I'd like a woollen pullover.
Ich möchte eine Hose aus Baumwolle.	I'd like a pair of cotton trousers.
Welche Größe?	Which size?
Mittelgroß.	Medium.
Haben Sie diese Krawatte in blau?	Have you got this tie in blue?
Ich möchte eine Sonnenbrille für meine kleine Schwester.	I'd like some sunglasses for my little sister.

Opening and closing times

die Geschäftszeiten	business hours
die Öffnungszeiten	opening times
geschlossen	closed
offen	open

aufmachen	to open
öffnen	to open
schließen	to close

Wann macht die Post auf?	When does the post office open?
Wann schließt der Supermarkt?	When does the supermarket close?
Sie ist bis vierzehn Uhr geschlossen.	It's closed until two o'clock.
Wann machen Sie zu?	When do you close?
Es ist Samstagnachmittag geschlossen.	It is closed on Saturday afternoons.

An welchen Tagen ist die Bank geschlossen?

Weight, volume, container

die Dose (-n)	tin		das Paket (-e)	packet
die Flasche (-n)	bottle		das Portemonnaie (-s)	purse
das Päckchen (-)	small packet		das Gramm	gram
die Schachtel (-n)	box		das Kilo	kilo
ein Stück	a piece		der Liter	litre
die Tasche (-n)	bag		das Pfund	pound
die Tüte (-n)	bag; carrier bag		pro Pfund	per pound
der Becher (-)	cup		ein paar	a few
die Brieftasche (-n)	wallet		einige	some
die Packung (-en)	package		voll	full

Eine Schachtel Pralinen, bitte.	A box of chocolates, please.
Ein Kilo Äpfel, bitte.	A kilo of apples, please.
Zweihundertfünfzig Gramm Käse, bitte.	250 grams of cheese, please.
Einen Liter Milch, bitte.	One litre of milk, please.
Ich möchte ein Stück Käse, bitte.	I'd like a piece of cheese, please.
Ein Pfund Tomaten, bitte.	A pound of tomatoes, please.
Haben Sie eine Flasche Weißwein?	Have you got a bottle of white wine?
Was kostet es pro Pfund?	What does it cost per pound?

Non-availability

einige	some; any		nicht mehr	no longer
leer	empty		noch etwas	any more
leider	unfortunately			

Haben Sie noch Brötchen?	Have you got any bread rolls left?
Wir haben keine Äpfel mehr.	We have no apples left.
Haben Sie noch Brot?	Have you got any bread left?
Wir haben leider kein Brot mehr.	Unfortunately we've got no bread.

Answer "Is that all?"

alles	everything; all		etwas	something; anything
auch	also			

Ist das alles?	Is that all?
Sonst noch etwas?	Anything else?
Nein, danke.	No, thank you.
Das wär's, danke.	That's all, thank you.

Opinions about clothes

breit	broad		teuer	expensive
eng	narrow		weit	wide
preiswert	cheap; good value		dies	this
riesig	enormous			

Wie gefällt dir mein Hemd?	How do you like my shirt?
Es ist sehr schön.	It's very nice.
Gefällt dir diese Hose?	Do you like these trousers?
Gefallen dir diese Schuhe?	Do you like these shoes?
Dieser Mantel ist sehr preiswert.	This coat is good value.
Die Krawatte ist mir zu breit.	The tie is too broad for me.

Buying something or not

Ich nehme diesen Mantel.	I'll take this coat.
Diese Hose ist mir zu groß.	These trousers are too large for me.
Diese Jacke ist mir zu kurz.	This jacket is too short for me.
Haben Sie etwas Kleineres?	Have you got anything smaller?
Haben Sie etwas Billigeres?	Have you got anything cheaper?

◀ *Public services* ▶

Ask where a post office or letter box is

der Briefkasten	letter box	**das Postamt (⸚er)**	post office

Wo gibt es eine Post?	Where is there a post office?
Gibt es eine Post hier in der Nähe?	Is there a post office near here?
Wo ist der Briefkasten?	Where is the letter box?
Vor der Post.	In front of the post office.

Sending a letter or postcard home

die Ansichts- **karte (-n)**	picture postcard	**Großbritannien**	Great Britain
der Brief (-e)	letter	**schicken**	to send

Ich möchte eine Ansichtskarte nach Großbritannien schicken.	I'd like to send a postcard to Great Britain.

Ask how much it costs to send letters or postcards

die Postkarte (-n)	postcard	**zusammen**	together

Was kostet es, einen Brief in die USA zu schicken?	What does it cost to send a letter to the USA?
Ich möchte diese Postkarte nach England schicken. Was kostet es?	I'd like to send this postcard to England. What does it cost?
Was macht das zusammen?	What does that cost altogether?

Ask for stamps

die Briefmarke (-n)   stamp

Eine Briefmarke zu achtzig Pfennig, bitte.	One stamp at 80 pfennig, please.
Ich möchte drei Briefmarken zu einer Mark, bitte.	I'd like three stamps at DM1, please.

Finding a telephone

der Marktplatz (-̈e)   market place   die Telefonzelle   public telephone box

Gibt es ein Telefon in der Nähe?	Is there a telephone nearby?
Es gibt eine Telefonzelle vor der Post.	There is a telephone in front of the post office.

◀ *Getting around* ▶

How to get into town

der Reisebus   coach   entlang   along
aussteigen   to get out   schnell   quick

Wie kommt man am besten in die Stadt?	What's the best way of getting to town?
Sie können mit dem Bus fahren.	You can go by bus.
Es ist schneller mit der U-Bahn.	It's quicker by underground.
Sie fahren diese Straße entlang.	You go along this road.

Understand simple signs and notices

Ausgang	exit
Auskunft	information
Abfahrt der Züge.	Train departures
Einstieg nur vorne.	Only get on at the front (of a bus or tram).
Kein Ausstieg.	No exit.
Ankunft der Züge.	Arrival times of trains.
Zu den Gleisen.	To the platforms.
der Ausstieg (-e)	exit
der Einstieg (-e)	entrance
der Nahverkehrszug	local train
der D-Zug	fast train
der Eilzug	fast train which stops at some stations
der Hauptbahnhof	main station
der Inter-City-Zug	Intercity train
die S-Bahn	an abbreviation for either "Schnellbahn" which is a fast train or "Stadtbahn" which is a suburban train.

der Werktag	working day
der Wochentag	weekday
aussteigen	to get out (of a vehicle)
einsteigen	to get into (a vehicle)

Getting to a particular place

die Linie	number (of bus or tram)		**der Zug (⁻e)**	train
die Straßenbahn	tram		**heute morgen**	this morning
			täglich	daily

Entschuldigen Sie, bitte. Fährt diese Straßenbahn in die Stadtmitte?	Excuse me. Does this tram go to the town centre?
Fährt heute morgen ein Zug nach Köln?	Is there a train to Cologne this morning?
Welche Linie fährt zum Bahnhof?	Which number (bus or tram) goes to the station?

Finding bus stops, toilets and platforms

die Auskunft	information		**der Fahrkarten-schalter (-)**	ticket office
der Bahnsteig (-e)	platform		**das Gepäck**	luggage
die Fahrkarte (-n)	ticket		**das Gleis (-e)**	platform
gleich	just			

Gibt es eine Straßenbahnhaltestelle hier in der Nähe?	Is there a tram stop near here?
Wo kann ich Fahrkarten kaufen?	Where can I buy tickets?
Wo ist die Auskunft?	Where is the information office?
Von welchem Gleis fährt der Zug nach München?	From which platform does the train to Munich go?
Die Haltestelle ist gleich um die Ecke.	The stop is just around the corner.

Was kann man am Fahrscheinautomat machen?

a. Man kann Getränke kaufen.
b. Man kann das Gepäck aufbewahren.
c. Man kann Fahrkarten kaufen.

Buying tickets

die Rückfahr-karte (-n)	return ticket		hin und zurück	return
der Zuschlag	supplementary fare		morgen früh	tomorrow morning
einfach	single		nach	to
			oder	or

Eine Rückfahrkarte nach Bonn, bitte.	A return ticket to Bonn, please.
Einfach oder hin und zurück?	A single or return?
Wann möchten Sie fahren?	When do you want to travel?
Morgen früh.	Tomorrow morning.
Welche Klasse?	Which class?
Zweite Klasse.	Second class.
Muß ich Zuschlag bezahlen?	Do I have to pay a supplement?

Times of arrival and departure

die Abfahrt (-en)	departure		abfahren	to leave
die Ankunft (÷e)	arrival		ankommen	to arrive
der Fahrplan	timetable		umsteigen	to change (trains)
Mitternacht	midnight		nächste	next

Wann fährt ein Zug nach Salzburg?	When is there a train to Salzburg?
Wann fährt der nächste Zug nach Zürich?	When does the next train go to Zürich?
Wann kommt er an?	When does it arrive?
Um elf Uhr zwanzig.	At 11.20 a.m.
Um zwanzig Uhr fünfundvierzig.	At 8.45 p.m. (20.45).
Muß ich umsteigen?	Do I have to change?
Nein, der Zug fährt direkt nach Bonn.	No, the train is a through train to Bonn.

Ticket checks

der Fahrschein (-e)	ticket		entwerten	to cancel (a ticket)
finden	to find		gratis	free

Ihre Fahrkarten, bitte.	Your tickets, please.
Ich kann meine Fahrkarte nicht finden.	I can't find my ticket.

Note: For buying fuel, breakdowns and accidents see pages 75-76.

Was kostet eine Fahrt mit dem City Bus?

THE WORLD OF WORK

◀ *Education and training* ▶

Future plans

das Abitur	final exam in German schools	**die Studentin (-nen)**	student (female)
der Beruf	profession; job	**die Uni(versität)**	university
die Hochschule (-n)	college	**nächstes Jahr**	next year
der Lehrling	apprentice	**bleiben**	to stay
die Oberstufe	sixth form	**sich interessieren (für)**	to be interested (in)
die Stelle (n)	job	**studieren**	to study
der Student (-en)	student (male)		

Was machst du nach dem Abitur?	What are you going to do after your final exams?
Ich werde nächstes Jahr auf die Hochschule gehen.	I'm going to college next year.
Ich bleibe auf der Schule.	I'm going to stay at school.
Ich möchte weiter studieren.	I would like to continue to study.
Ich möchte eine Stelle als Lehrling finden.	I would like to find a job as an apprentice.

◀ *Careers and employment* ▶

Travelling to work

Berufe	**Jobs**		
der Apotheker (-)	chemist (male)	**die Kellnerin (-nen)**	waitress
die Apotheke-rin (-nen)	chemist (female)	**die Kranken-schwester (-n)**	nurse (female)
der Bäcker (-)	baker (male)	**der Kranken-pfleger (-)**	nurse (male)
die Bäckerin (-nen)	baker (female)	**der Lehrer (-)**	teacher (male)
der Bauer (-n)	farmer (male)	**die Lehrerin (-nen)**	teacher (female)
die Bäuerin (-nen)	farmer (female)	**der Mechaniker (-)**	mechanic (male)
der Beamte (-n)	civil servant, official (male)	**die Mechanike-rin (-nen)**	mechanic (female)
die Beamtin (-nen)	civil servant, official (female)	**der Metzger (-)**	butcher (male)
der Busfahrer (-)	bus driver (male)	**die Metzgerin (-nen)**	butcher (female)
die Busfahre-rin (-nen)	bus driver (female)	**der Sekretär (-)**	secretary (male)
der Friseur	hairdresser (male)	**die Sekretärin (-nen)**	secretary (female)
die Friseurin	hairdresser (female)	**der Schauspieler (-)**	actor
die Hausfrau (-en)	housewife	**die Schauspiele-rin (-nen)**	actress
der Geschäfts-mann (¨er)	businessman	**der Schüler (-)**	schoolboy
die Geschäfts-frau (-en)	businesswoman	**die Schülerin (-nen)**	schoolgirl
der Kellner (-)	waiter	**der Verkäufer (-)**	salesman
		die Verkäufe-rin (-nen)	saleswoman

die Arbeit	work
die Fahrt (-en)	journey
eine Viertelstunde	a quarter of an hour
etwa	approximately
Wie kommst du zur Arbeit?	How do you get to work?
Ich komme normalerweise mit dem Auto.	I usually come by car.
Die Reise dauert etwa eine Viertelstunde.	The journey takes about quarter of an hour.

Out of work

arbeitslos unemployed	**die Arbeitslosigkeit** unemployment

Was macht dein Bruder?	What does your brother do?
Er ist arbeitslos.	He's unemployed.
Er kann keine Stelle finden.	He can't find a job.
Er möchte eine Stelle als Bäcker.	He would like to work as a baker.
Es ist nicht einfach, so eine Stelle zu finden.	It's not easy to find such a job.

Jobs and work experience

das Arbeits-praktikum work experience	**der Job (-s)** job
das Büro (-s) office	**die Firma (Firmen)** company
die Fabrik (-en) factory	**arbeiten** to work
	austragen to deliver

Was macht sie?	What does she do?
Sie arbeitet in einer Fabrik.	She works in a factory.
Er arbeitet in einem Büro.	He works in an office.
Sie arbeitet bei Ford.	She works for Ford.
Hast du einen Job?	Have you got a job?
Ja, ich trage Zeitungen aus.	Yes, I deliver newspapers.
Am Wochenende arbeite ich als Kellnerin.	I work as a waitress at the weekend.
Hast du ein Arbeitspraktikum gemacht?	Have you done work experience?
Ja, ich habe drei Wochen in einer Fabrik gearbeitet.	Yes, I worked for three weeks in a factory.

Spare time jobs

bekommen to get	**verdienen** to earn
halbtags half-day	

Arbeitest du am Wochenende?	Do you work at weekends?
Ja, samstags arbeite ich vier Stunden.	Yes, I work for four hours on Saturday.
Ich arbeite nicht.	I don't work.
Ich arbeite als Babysitter.	I work as a babysitter.
Ich verdiene drei Pfund pro Stunde.	I earn £3 an hour.
Ich arbeite seit zwei Monaten in einem Supermarkt.	I've been working in a supermarket for two months.
Ich arbeite nur halbtags.	I just work for half days.

Opinions about jobs

Ich finde es sehr interessant.	I find it very interesting.
Es ist langweilig, aber ich brauche das Geld.	It's boring but I need the money.
Ich möchte später so eine Stelle finden.	I'd like to find a job like that later on.

Jobs – yourself and your family

Mein Vater ist Busfahrer.	My father is a busdriver.
Meine Mutter ist Beamtin.	My mother is a civil servant.
Meine Schwester ist Polizistin.	My sister is a policewoman.
Ich möchte Krankenschwester werden.	I'd like to become a nurse.
Meine Tante war früher Lehrerin.	My aunt used to be a teacher.

◀ *Advertising and publicity* ▶

Advertisements

die Anzeige (-n)	advertisement		**die Werbung**	advertisement
das Bild (-er)	picture		**komisch**	funny

Ich finde dieses Bild besonders gut.	I think this picture is particularly good.
Ich finde diese Werbung ziemlich komisch.	I think this advert rather funny.
Ich finde dieses Foto wirklich häßlich.	I think this photo is really ugly.

Publicity

ausverkauft	sold out		**das Sonder-**	special offer
			angebot (-e)	

Die neuen CDs sind alle ausverkauft.	The new CDs have all been sold out.
Die Jeans sind im Sonderangebot.	The jeans are on special offer.

Normalerweise kostet ein T-Shirt DM10. Was kostet es heute?

Ab sofort auf alle Waren noch 10% Rabatt

◀ *Communication* ▶

Telephone numbers

die Telefon-nummer (-n)	phone number	die Vorwahl	dialling code

Wie ist Ihre Telefonnummer?	What is your phone number?
Zweiundsechzig, achtundfünfzig, sechsundneunzig.	62 58 96.
Kennen Sie die Vorwahl?	Do you know the dialling code?

Answer a telephone call

Claudia am Apparat.	Claudia speaking.
Hallo. Schmidt.	Hello. This is Schmidt speaking.

Ask to speak to someone

der Augenblick	moment	da	there
der Moment	moment		

Ich möchte bitte Frau Schäfer sprechen.	I'd like to speak to Mrs. Schäfer, please.
Kann ich Herrn Meyer sprechen, bitte?	May I speak to Mr. Meyer, please?
Ist Klaus da?	Is Klaus there?
Einen Augenblick, bitte.	One moment, please.

Telephone messages

anrufen	to phone	zurückrufen	to call back
ausrichten	to leave a message	möglich	possible
telefonieren	to phone	sofort	at once
verbinden	to connect	zwischen	between
versuchen	to try		

Ich versuche, Sie zu verbinden.	I'm trying to connect you.
Das ist nicht möglich.	That's not possible.
Können Sie ihm etwas ausrichten?	Can I leave a message for him?
Kann ich ihm etwas ausrichten?	Would you like to leave him a message?
Sagen Sie ihm, daß Frau Meyer angerufen hat.	Tell him that Mrs. Meyer phoned.
Kann er mich zurückrufen?	Can he call me back?
Meine Nummer ist achtzehn fünfund-siebzig null zwo*.	My number is 18 75 02.
Wann soll er zurückrufen?	When should he call back?
Zwischen vierzehn und fünfzehn Uhr.	Between 2pm and 3pm.

*People often say "zwo" instead of "zwei" on the telephone.

Say what sort of room

das Bad bath	**was für?** what kind of?
die Dusche (-n) shower	

Was für ein Zimmer?	What kind of room?
Ich möchte ein Einzelzimmer mit Bad.	I'd like a single room with a bath.
Ich habe ein Doppelzimmer mit Dusche reserviert.	I've reserved a double room with a shower.

Ask the cost

Halbpension half-board	**das Zelt (-e)** tent
Vollpension full-board	

Was kostet es pro Person?	What does it cost per person?
Was kostet es für eine Nacht für ein Zelt?	What does it cost for one night for a tent?
Was kostet ein Zimmer mit Bad?	What does a room with a bath cost?
Was kostet Vollpension?	What does full-board cost?

Accept or reject the accommodation

billig cheap	**teuer** expensive
etwas anything	

Es ist mir zu teuer.	It's too expensive for me.
Haben Sie etwas Billigeres?	Have you got anything cheaper?
Gut. Ich nehme das Zimmer.	Good. I'll take the room.

Identify yourself

Ich habe ein Zimmer reserviert.	I've reserved a room.
Mein Name ist Meyer.	My name is Meyer.
Wir haben schon reserviert.	We have already made a reservation.
Wir sind drei, zwei Mädchen und ein Junge.	There are three of us, two girls and a boy.

Ask where facilities are

Entschuldigen Sie, bitte. Excuse me, please.	**der Schlüssel (-)** key
der Lift (-e or -s) lift	**der Spielplatz (⁻e)** play area
	die Toilette toilet

Entschuldigen Sie, bitte. Wo sind die Toiletten?	Excuse me please, where are the toilets?
Sie sind hier links.	They are here on the left.
Wo ist das Restaurant?	Where is the restaurant?
Gibt es einen Spielplatz?	Is there a play area?
Ja, hinter dem Hotel.	Yes, behind the hotel.

Paying

die Rechnung (-en) bill	**die Übernachtung** overnight accommodation

Ich hätte gern die Rechnung, bitte.	I would like the bill, please.
Was kostet eine Übernachtung?	What does overnight accommodation cost?
Ich möchte zahlen, bitte.	I'd like to pay, please.

Book accommodation

ankommen to arrive **gegen** at about	**die Woche (-n)** week

Ich möchte ein Zimmer für den vierten Mai reservieren.	I would like to reserve a room for the 4th of May.
Wir kommen gegen achtzehn Uhr an.	We will arrive at about 6 p.m.
Ich möchte ein Einzelzimmer mit Halbpension für eine Woche reservieren.	I would like to book a single room with half-board for a week.

Note: For youth hostels and campsites see page 84.

Meal times

Wann ist Frühstück?	When is breakfast?
Zwischen acht Uhr und neun Uhr dreißig.	Between 8 o'clock and 9.30.
Das Mittagessen ist von zwölf Uhr bis vierzehn Uhr.	Lunch is from 12 o'clock to 2 o'clock.
Das Abendessen beginnt um neunzehn Uhr.	Dinner starts at 7 p.m.
Das Restaurant ist am Dienstag geschlossen.	The restaurant is closed on Tuesday.

Lies diesen Brief und beantworte die Fragen.

1. Was für Zimmer hat Frau Braun reserviert?
2. Wie viele Nächte möchte sie bleiben?

HOTEL RESTAURANT-CAFÉ ALEMANNENHOF

Frau Braun
Bahnhofstr. 56
Wuppertal

5. Mai

Ihre Reservierung für 1 Doppelzimmer/Bad.

Sehr geehrte Frau Braun!

Wir danken für Ihre Reservierung, die wir hiermit bestätigen:

1 Doppelzimmer/Bad vom 21. bis 22. Juli.

Preis: per Doppelzimmer/Nacht **DM130**
(inklusive Frühstückbuffet).

Wir freuen uns schon, Sie bei uns willkommen heißen zu dürfen und
werden uns bemühen, Ihnen einen angenehmen Aufenthalt bei uns zu
bieten.

N. Forst

Familie Forst

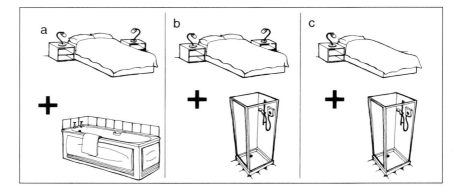

◀ *The wider world* ▶

Understand the names of countries and nationalities commonly encountered

Afrika	Africa	**der Süden**	South
Amerika	America	**der Westen**	West
Belgien	Belgium	**die Alpen**	Alps
die Bundesrepublik	Germany	**die Nordsee**	North Sea
Deutschland		**die Ostsee**	Baltic
Dänemark	Denmark	**der Rhein**	Rhine
EU	European Union	**Köln**	Cologne
Frankreich	France	**München**	Munich
Griechenland	Greece	**Wien**	Vienna
Großbritannien	Great Britain		
Holland	Holland	**der Amerikaner (-)**	American man
Irland	Ireland	**die Amerika-**	American woman
Italien	Italy	**nerin (-nen)**	
die Niederlande	Netherlands	**der Deutsche (-n)**	German man
Norwegen	Norway	**die Deutsche (-n)**	German woman
Österreich	Austria	**der Franzose (-n)**	Frenchman
Polen	Poland	**die Französin (-nen)**	French woman
Rumänien	Rumania	**der Holländer (-)**	Dutchman
Rußland	Russia	**die Holländerin**	Dutch woman
Schottland	Scotland	**(-nen)**	
Schweden	Sweden	**der Italiener (-)**	Italian man
die Schweiz	Switzerland	**die Italienerin (-nen)**	Italian woman
die Slowakei	Slovakia	**der Österreicher (-)**	Austrian man
Spanien	Spain	**die Österreicherin**	Austrian woman
die Tsche-	Czech republic	**(-nen)**	
chische Republik		**der Schweizer (-)**	Swiss man
die Türkei	Turkey	**die Schweizerin**	Swiss woman
Ungarn	Hungary	**(-nen)**	
die USA	USA	**der Spanier (-)**	Spaniard
der Norden	North	**die Spanierin (-nen)**	Spanish woman
der Osten	East	**jemals**	ever

Ich war in der Türkei.	I was in Turkey.
Meine Großeltern wohnen in der Schweiz.	My grandparents live in Switzerland.
Warst du jemals in Rußland?	Have you ever been to Russia?
Mein Vater ist Holländer.	My father is Dutch.

◀ *Examination German* ▶

Rubrics and instructions

Bitte ausfüllen.	Please fill in.
Unterstreiche.	Underline.
Kreuze an.	Mark with a cross.
Schreib die richtige Nummer (auf den Plan).	Write the correct number (on the plan).
Schreib die richtigen Namen/Nummern neben die Bilder.	Write the correct names/numbers next to the pictures.
Schreib an deinen Brieffreund/deine Brieffreundin.	Write to your penfriend.
Schreib einen Brief an ...	Write a letter to ...
Schreib einen Bericht über ...	Write a report about ...
Beantworte (die Fragen).	Answer (the questions).
Beschreib.	Describe.
Erklär.	Explain.
Finde.	Find.
Sag.	Say.
Schau ... an.	Look at ...
Frag.	Ask.
Was ist richtig?	What is right?
Was ist falsch?	What is wrong?
Was bedeuten diese Symbole?	What do these symbols mean?
Lies den Text und füll die Lücken in den folgenden Sätzen aus.	Read the text and fill in the gaps in the following sentences.
Lies den Artikel.	Read the article.
Schreib ... positive/negative Sätze.	Write ... positive/negative sentences.
Ordne die Sätze/Bilder.	Put the sentences/pictures in order.
Wähl ...	Choose ...
Schreib/sag deine Meinung zu/über ...	Write/say your opinion about ...
Gib Information über ...	Give information about ...
Stell Fragen über ...	Ask questions about ...
Was paßt zusammen?	What matches?

◀ *Question Words* ▶

wann	when		wieso	why
warum	why		wieviel	how much
was	what		wie viele	how many
welche	which		wo	where
wer	who		woher	where from
wie	how		wohin	where to

◀ *Abbreviations* ▶

d.h.	i.e.		Str.	Street
einschl.	including		usw.	etc.
gem.	mixed		WC	W.C.
inbegr.	including		z.B.	e.g.
inkl.	including			

HIGHER TIER

EVERYDAY ACTIVITIES

◀ *Language of the classroom* ▶

Explain a word

das Ding (-e)	thing	**erklären**	to explain
das Wort (ᵉer)	word		

Könnten Sie dieses Wort erklären, bitte?	Could you explain this word, please?
Wie heißt das Ding da?	What's that thing called?

How is it pronounced?

aussprechen	to pronounce

Wie sagt man dieses Wort?	How do you say this word?
Wie spricht man das aus?	How do you pronounce that?
Wie spricht man diesen Ausdruck aus?	How do you pronounce this expression?

Classroom activities

die Gruppe (-n)	group	**diskutieren**	to discuss
der Haken (-)	tick	**ergänzen**	to complete
die Spalte (-n)	column	**fehlen**	to be missing
die Tabelle (-n)	grid	**eine Frage stellen**	to ask a question
die Umfrage (-n)	survey	**vergleichen**	to compare
austeilen	to hand out		

Arbeitest du mit mir?	Will you work with me?
Wer beginnt?	Who is going to start?
Ich bin dran.	It's my turn.
Jetzt bist du dran.	Now it's your turn.
Teil bitte die Hefte aus.	Hand the books out, please.
Markiere die Sätze mit einem Haken.	Tick the sentences.
Tragt eure Antworten in die Tabelle ein.	Enter your answers on the grid.
Vergleicht eure Antworten.	Compare your answers.

◀ *School* ▶

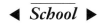

Learning languages

die Sprache (-n)	language	**Russisch**	Russian
die Fremd-	foreign language	**die Zeit**	time
sprache (-n)		**andere**	other
Italienisch	Italian	**fließend**	fluently

Welche Fremdsprachen lernst du?	Which foreign languages are you learning?
Seit wann lernst du Deutsch?	For how long have you been learning German?
Ich lerne seit vier Jahren Deutsch.	I've been learning German for four years.
Kannst du auch andere Sprachen?	Can you also speak other languages?
Ich spreche fließend Spanisch.	I speak Spanish fluently.
Ich möchte Russisch lernen.	I'd like to learn Russian.

School timetables, terms and holidays

die Ganztags-schule (-n)	full-day school	der Stunden-plan (¨e)	timetable
die Halbtags-schule (-n)	mornings only at school	das Trimester (-)	school term (three in one year)
das Schuljahr	school year	schwer	hard
das Semester (-)	school term (two in one year)		

Ich finde, die Tage sind zu lang.	I think the days are too long.
Was meinst du?	What do you think?
Das stimmt vielleicht.	Perhaps you're right.
Ich bin derselben Meinung.	I agree.
Ich möchte lieber eine Halbtagsschule.	I would prefer mornings only at school.
Ich mag das dritte Trimester am liebsten.	I like the third term best.

School subjects, rules and uniform

die Regel (-n)	rule	etwas für richtig halten	to agree with something
die Schulordnung	school rules	tragen	to wear
das Recht	the right	blöd	stupid
die Schuluniform	school uniform	nützlich	useful
die Strafe (-n)	punishment	nutzlos	useless
die Oberstufe	sixth form	praktisch	practical
das Pflichtfach (¨er)	compulsory subject	völlig	completely
das Wahlfach (¨er)	optional subject		
nachsitzen	to be in detention		

Meiner Meinung nach gibt es zu viele Pflichtfächer.	In my opinion there are too many compulsory subjects.
Ich meine, man sollte nicht so viele Fächer machen müssen.	I think you shouldn't have to do so many subjects.
Was darf man in der Schule nicht machen?	What are you not allowed to do at school?
Ich finde es richtig, daß man nicht rauchen darf.	I think it's right that you shouldn't be allowed to smoke.

Ich finde es doof, daß man in der Schule keinen Mantel tragen darf.	I think it's stupid that we are not allowed to wear coats in school.
Bist du für oder gegen eine Schuluniform?	Are you for or against a school uniform?
Ich finde, daß eine Schuluniform gut ist, weil es praktisch und billig ist.	I think a school uniform is good because it is practical and cheap.
Ich werde es nie für richtig halten, daß man eine Uniform tragen muß.	I'll never agree with wearing a uniform.
Ich finde eine Schuluniform völlig blöd, weil sie teuer und so altmodisch ist.	I think a school uniform is completely stupid because it is expensive and so old-fashioned.

Information about schools

die Grundschule (-n)	primary school	**sitzenbleiben**	to stay in the same class for another year
das Internat	boarding school	**gemischt**	mixed
die Klassen-arbeit (-en)	class test	**hitzefrei**	no school because of hot weather
SMV	student council	**schulfrei**	no school
das Zeugnis (-se)	school report	**schneefrei**	no school because of snow
bestehen	to pass an exam		
durchfallen	to fail		
schwänzen	to play truant		

German exams are marked in the following way (1 is the highest mark):

1 = sehr gut	very good		**4 = ausreichend**	satisfactory
2 = gut	good		**5 = mangelhaft**	poor
3 = befriedigend	fair		**6 = ungenügend**	unsatisfactory

Wenn man nicht fleißig arbeitet, bleibt man sitzen.	If you don't work hard you have to repeat the year.
Wenn es sehr heiß ist, hat man hitzefrei.	If the weather becomes very hot there is no school.
Es gibt nicht sehr viele Gesamtschulen.	There are not very many comprehensive schools.
Ich finde gemischte Schulen gut.	I think mixed schools are good.
Es ist normal, mit Jungen (Mädchen) zu arbeiten.	It's normal to work with boys (girls).
Ich kann in einer gemischten Klasse nicht gut arbeiten.	I can't work well in a mixed class.

? Lies diesen Brief und die Antwort und beantworte die Fragen.

Krank am Dienstag

Wir haben in der Woche eine Doppelstunde Geschichte, und die am Mittwoch. An einem Mittwoch besuchte ich den Unterricht, war aber am darauffolgenden Dienstag krank und konnte deshalb nachmittags nicht lernen. Am Mittwoch bin ich dann wieder zur Schule gegangen, wurde in Geschichte abgefragt und bekam eine Vier. Da ich mich mit dieser Note nicht zufriedengebe, möchte ich wissen, ob ich meinen Lehrer zu diesem Fall befragen kann.

Anna

Antwort

Wie die Note Vier beweist, warst Du bei der Prüfung ja nicht völlig blank. Ich kann nicht beurteilen, ob Deine Kenntnisse noch von der letzten Unterrichtsstunde herrührten, oder ob eine direkte häusliche Vorbereitung auf die Stunde notwendig war. Jedenfalls hatte der Lehrer das Recht. Es bestand keine dringende Notwendigkeit, daß Du Dich erst am Nachmittag vorher auf den Geschichtsunterricht vorbereitest. Das hättest Du schon früher tun können.

Claudia Schmidt

1. Warum ist Anna nicht glücklich?
2. Was steht in Claudias Antwort?
   a. Sie soll es mit dem Lehrer besprechen.
   b. Sie soll sich nicht nur am Abend vor der Klassenarbeit vorbereiten.
   c. Ihre Eltern sollen mit dem Lehrer sprechen.

◀ *Home life* ▶

Typical meals, meal times and eating habits

das Fleisch	meat	die Gurke (-n)	cucumber
die Forelle	trout	der Kohl	cabbage
das Kalbfleisch	veal	das Sauerkraut	pickled cabbage
Wurst und Käse	selection of cold sausages and cheese	die (Wein-) traube (-n)	grape
das Rindfleisch	beef	die Zitrone (-n)	lemon
der Schweinebraten	roast pork	die Zwiebel (-n)	onion
der Blumenkohl	cauliflower	der Knödel (-)	dumpling
die Birne (-n)	pear	die (Schlag)sahne	(whipped) cream
die Erbse (-n)	pea	das Spiegelei (-er)	fried egg

Abends essen wir normalerweise Wurst und Käse.	In the evening we usually eat a selection of cold sausages and cheese.
Ich esse kein Fleisch.	I don't eat meat.
Wir essen nicht gern spät am Abend.	We don't like eating late in the evening.

Helping around the house

abräumen	to clear the table	staubsaugen	to vacuum
abwaschen	to wash up	vorbereiten	to prepare
bügeln	to iron	das Geschirr	dishes
einkaufen gehen	to go shopping	die Spülmaschine	dishwasher
putzen	to clean	der Topf (¨e)	pan

Wie kann ich Ihnen helfen?	How can I help you?
Könntest du den Tisch decken?	Could you set the table?
Ich könnte staubsaugen.	I could vacuum.
Tu das Geschirr in die Spülmaschine.	Put the dishes in the dishwasher.
Ich habe schon abgewaschen.	I've already done the washing-up.
Wenn Sie wollen, könnte ich einkaufen gehen.	If you like I could go shopping.

How members of the family help at home

mähen	to mow	der Rasen	lawn

Bei uns macht meine Mutter die Hausarbeit.	My mother does the housework in our house.
Mein Vater bereitet immer das Abendessen vor.	My father always prepares the evening meal.
Mein Bruder hilft immer in der Küche.	My brother always helps in the kitchen.
Gestern habe ich den Rasen gemäht.	I mowed the lawn yesterday.

Say if you share a room

eigene	own	Pech haben	to be unlucky
Glück haben	to be lucky	teilen	to share

Ich habe mein eigenes Zimmer.	I have my own room.
Du hast aber Glück!	You're lucky!
Ich teile mein Zimmer mit meinem Bruder.	I share my room with my brother.
Ich möchte sehr gern mein eigenes Zimmer haben.	I'd very much like to have my own room.

◄ *Media* ►

Narrate a theme or plot of a book

der Detektiv (-e)	detective		stattfinden	to take place
der Held (-en)	hero		töten	to kill
die Heldin (-nen)	heroine		sich verlieben	to fall in love
der Roman (-e)	novel		allmählich	gradually
der Schriftsteller (-)	author		am Anfang	at the beginning
es handelt sich um + Akk.	it's about		neulich	recently

Liest du gern?	Do you like reading?
Ja, ich habe neulich einen sehr guten Roman gelesen.	Yes, I recently read a very good novel.
Worum handelt es sich?	What is it about?
Es findet in Berlin statt.	It takes place in Berlin.
Am Anfang wird eine Frau getötet.	At the beginning a woman is killed.
Allmählich verlieben sie sich.	Gradually they fall in love.

Narrate a simple item of news

in Streik treten	to go on strike		der Unfall (⁼e)	accident
der Krieg	war			

Hast du gehört, was gestern passiert ist?	Did you hear what happened yesterday?
Ich habe die Nachrichten im Fernsehen gesehen.	I saw the news on television.
Ein schwerer Unfall ist passiert.	There has been a serious accident.
Hier steht, daß morgen die Bahnbeamten in Streik treten werden.	It says here that the railway workers will be on strike tomorrow.

Newspapers, magazines, books, TV programmes, radio, music and performers

hassen	to hate

Hast du die neue CD gehört?	Have you heard the new CD?
Was ist deine Lieblingsgruppe?	What is your favourite group?
Hast du die Sendung gestern abend gesehen?	Did you see the programme last night?
Was meinst du?	What do you think?
Ich hasse die Sendung.	I hate the programme.
Ich lese nie die Zeitungen.	I never read the newspapers.

Narrate the main features of a TV or radio programme

der Bericht (-e)	report	das Kranken-	hospital
der Dokumentar-	documentary	haus (¨er)	
film (-e)		die Krimiserie	detective series
die Fernseh-	television serial	die Tagesschau	news
serie (-n)		der Trickfilm (-e)	cartoon
		berühmt	famous

Es handelt sich um junge Leute, die in Australien wohnen.	It's about young people who live in Australia.
Es bespricht Jugendprobleme.	It discusses young people's problems.
Man interviewt berühmte Leute.	Famous people are interviewed.
Es spielt in einem Krankenhaus.	It takes place in a hospital.

◀ *Health and fitness* ▶

Arrange to consult a doctor, dentist or chemist

der Arzt (¨e)	doctor (male)	das Sprech-	surgery
die Ärztin (-nen)	doctor (female)	zimmer (-)	
der Notdienst	emergency service	der Termin (-e)	appointment
die Sprech-	consultation	der Zahnarzt (¨e)	dentist
stunde (-n)		dringend	urgent
		ernst	serious

Ich habe mich beim Arzt angemeldet.	I've made an appointment with the doctor.
Ich möchte einen Termin mit dem Zahnarzt.	I would like an appointment with the dentist.
Kann ich den Zahnarzt sprechen?	Can I see the dentist?
Wann möchten Sie kommen?	When would you like to come?
Ich brauche einen Termin für heute.	I must have an appointment today.

Wann kann man keinen Termin bei diesem Arzt vereinbaren?

Dr. med. Heide-Erika Weber
Dr. med. Gerda Kraft

Sprechstunden:
Mo., Di., Mi., Fr., 8⁰⁰-12⁰⁰ Uhr
Do. vorm. nach Vereinbarung
Mo., Di. 16³⁰-18⁰⁰ Uhr
Do.16⁰⁰-19³⁰ Uhr
Fr. 15³⁰-17⁰⁰ Uhr

Mi. Nachmittag keine Sprechstunde

At a doctor's, dentist's or chemist's

das Knie (-)	knee	der Sonnenbrand	sunburn
der Mund	mouth	brechen	to break
das Hansaplast	sticking plaster	empfehlen	to recommend
das Medika-ment (-e)	medicine	sich hinlegen	to lie down
		sich weh tun	to hurt oneself
das Rezept (-e)	prescription	schneiden	to cut
der Saft	syrup	stechen	to sting
eine Salbe	a cream	sterben	to die
die Spritze (-n)	injection	tot	dead
eine Tablette	tablet	sich übergeben	to be sick
der Teelöffel (-)	teaspoon	verbrennen	to burn
der Husten	cough	verletzt	injured

Ich habe mich am Arm verbrannt.	I've burnt my arm.
Ich glaube, er hat sich das Bein gebrochen.	I think he's broken his leg.
Ich habe einen Sonnenbrand.	I'm sunburnt.
Ich empfehle diese Tabletten.	I recommend these tablets.
Nehmen Sie die Tabletten zweimal am Tag nach dem Essen.	Take the tablets twice a day after meals.
Ich bin hingefallen.	I fell down.

Healthy and unhealthy lifestyles

der Alkohol	alcohol	die Zigarette (-n)	cigarette
das Essen	food	der Tabak	tobacco
die Kalorie (-n)	calorie		
der Raucher (-)	smoker	abnehmen	to lose weight
der Nichtraucher (-)	non-smoker	aufwachen	to wake up
die Abhängigkeit	dependance	einschlafen	to fall asleep
die Sucht (¨e) (nach)	addiction (to)	folgen	to follow
		rauchen	to smoke
die Nikotinsucht	nicotine addiction	aufstehen	to get up
die Rauschgiftsucht	drug addiction	vermeiden	to avoid
die Trunksucht	alcohol addiction	versuchen	to try
der Rauschgiftmiß-brauch	drug abuse	fett	fat, greasy
		süchtig	addicted
der/die Süchtige (-r)	addict	alkoholsüchtig	alcoholic
der/die Sucht-kranke(-r)	addict		

Man soll viel Sport treiben.	You should do a lot of sport.
Man soll fettes Essen vermeiden.	You should avoid fatty food.
Ich versuche, während der Woche nicht zu spät ins Bett zu gehen.	I try not to go to bed too late during the week.
Ich stehe immer früh auf.	I always get up early.
Was machst du, um fit zu bleiben?	What do you do to keep fit?
Ich gehe jeden Tag schwimmen.	I go swimming every day.

◀ *Food* ▶

React to offers of food and drink, giving reasons

der Eintopf	stew	**der Sekt**	sparkling wine
das Gebäck	biscuits	**die Soße**	gravy
das Kotelett (-s)	chop	**allergisch gegen**	allergic to
das Lammfleisch	lamb	**+ Akk.**	
der Pudding	blancmange	**reichen**	to be enough

Noch ein paar Zwiebeln?	A few more onions?
Nein, danke. Das reicht.	No thank you. That's enough.
Ja, bitte. Sie schmecken sehr gut.	Yes, please. They taste very good.
Ich bin gegen Erdbeeren allergisch.	I'm allergic to strawberries.
Ich habe Sauerkraut nie probiert.	I've never tried pickled cabbage.
Ich möchte es sehr gern probieren.	I'd like to try it.
Ich darf keine Eier essen.	I'm not allowed to eat eggs.

Appreciation and compliments

ausgezeichnet	excellent	**die Köchin (-nen)**	chef, cook (female)
der Koch (¨e)	chef, cook (male)	**gratulieren**	to congratulate

Ich gratuliere dem Koch.	Please give my compliments to the chef.
Ich gratuliere.	Congratulations.
Ich werde dieses Essen nie vergessen.	I'll never forget this meal.
Vielen Dank für ein ausgezeichnetes Essen.	Thank you very much for an excellent meal.

Ask for food and table items

die Schüssel (-n)	bowl	**die Untertasse (-n)**	saucer
der Teller (-)	plate		

Möchten Sie noch etwas Torte?	Would you like some more cream cake?
Brauchen Sie eine Schüssel?	Do you need a bowl?
Kann ich eine Schüssel haben, bitte?	May I have a bowl, please?

Ask for more or say that you have had enough

Gibt es noch etwas Fleisch?	Is there any more meat?
Ich esse so gern Pudding.	I like blancmange so much.
Schmeckt's?	Do you like it?
Fisch schmeckt mir immer gut.	I always like fish.
Wir hätten gern noch eine Flasche Mineralwasser.	We would like another bottle of mineral water.
Ich habe schon zu viel gegessen.	I've already eaten too much.

Ask for a table

die Person (-en)	person	reservieren	to reserve

Wie viele sind Sie denn?	How many of you are there?
Wir sind fünf Personen.	There are five of us.
Haben Sie einen Tisch für zwei?	Have you got a table for two?
Ich möchte einen Tisch für vier Personen reservieren.	I'd like to reserve a table for four people.

State preference for seating

draußen	outside	im Schatten	in the shade
drinnen	inside	die Terrasse	terrace
Nichtraucher	no smoking		

Haben Sie einen Tisch am Fenster?	Have you got a table at the window?
Wir möchten draußen essen.	We'd like to eat outside.
Wir möchten lieber im Schatten sitzen.	We would prefer to sit in the shade.

Complain, giving reasons

sich beschweren	to complain	der Chef	the manager
bestellen	to order	zufrieden	satisfied

Wir haben keinen Salat bestellt.	We didn't order salad.
Ich möchte mit dem Chef sprechen.	I'd like to speak to the manager.
Ich möchte mich beim Chef beschweren.	I'd like to complain to the manager.
Ich habe ein Schweinekotelett und kein Kalbskotelett bestellt.	I ordered a pork chop not a veal chop.
Wir mußten lange auf das Essen warten.	We had to wait a long time for our meal.
Als man mir endlich die Suppe gebracht hat, war sie kalt.	When they eventually brought me the soup it was cold.
Ich bin gar nicht zufrieden.	I'm not at all satisfied.

Ask about service charges

die Bedienung	service	inbegriffen	included
das Trinkgeld	tip	inklusive	included
einschließlich	included		

Ist das inklusive Bedienung?	Is the service charge included?
Sind die Getränke inbegriffen?	Are the drinks included?
Alles ist inbegriffen.	Everything is included.

PERSONAL AND SOCIAL LIFE

◀ *Self, family and friends* ▶

State, and understand others stating, gender and marital status

der Cousin (-s)	cousin (male)	der Witwer (-)	widower
die Cousine (-n)	cousin (female)	die Witwe (-n)	widow
das Ehepaar (-e)	married couple	heiraten	to marry
der Enkel (-)	grandson	geschieden	divorced
die Enkelin (-nen)	granddaughter	getrennt	separated
die Frau (-en)	wife	ledig	single; unmarried
der Mann (¨er)	husband	männlich	male
der Neffe (-n)	nephew	weiblich	female
die Nichte (-n)	niece	unverheiratet	unmarried
die Stiefmutter (¨)	stepmother	verlobt	engaged
der Verwandte (-n)	relative		

Meine älteste Schwester hat zwei Kinder.	My eldest sister has two children.
Mein Bruder ist nicht verheiratet.	My brother is not married.
Meine Eltern sind seit zwei Jahren geschieden.	My parents have been divorced for two years.

Spell out names, streets and towns

der Bezirk (-e)	district	das Land (¨er)	state; province
die Heimat-stadt (¨e)	home town		

Wie schreibt man deinen Straßennamen?	How do you write the name of your street?
Könnten Sie den Namen von Ihrer Stadt buchstabieren?	Could you spell the name of your town?

Describe character and personality

ehrlich	honest	ruhig	calm
frech	cheeky	schlecht gelaunt	in a bad mood
höflich	polite	schüchtern	shy
gut gelaunt	in a good mood	sympathisch	likeable
lebhaft	lively	vernünftig	sensible
neugierig	curious	sich verlassen auf	to rely on
nervös	nervous		

Wie gefällt dir Ralf?	How do you like Ralf?
Ich finde ihn ein bißchen zu lebhaft.	I find him a bit too lively.
Ich ärgere mich über Klaus, weil er immer schlecht gelaunt ist.	Klaus annoys me because he's always in a bad mood.

Express feelings about others

auskommen mit + Dat.	to get on with	sich Sorgen machen um + Akk.	to worry about
es gelingt mir	I succeed	der Nachbar (-n)	neighbour (male)
lächeln	to smile	die Nachbarin (-nen)	neighbour (female)
scheinen	to seem	seltsam	strange
sich vertragen mit + Dat.	to get along well with	traurig	sad
		überraschend	surprising

Wie kommst du mit deinen Eltern aus?	How do you get on with your parents?
Ich komme mit ihnen gut aus.	I get on well with them.
Claudia scheint sehr vernünftig zu sein.	Claudia seems to be very sensible.
Man kann sich auf sie verlassen.	You can rely on her.
Ich vertrage mich gut mit meinem Bruder.	I get on well with my brother.
Ich kann sie nicht leiden.	I can't stand her.
Ich bin sicher, daß es ihm gelingen wird.	I'm sure he will succeed.
Ich mache mir Sorgen um ihn.	I'm worried about him.

◄ *Free time, holidays and special occasions* ►

Hobbies, interests and leisure activities

Schach spielen	to play chess	die Sammlung (-en)	collection
Schlittschuh laufen	to skate	die Welt	world
segeln	to sail	außer	except for
eine Wanderung machen	to go walking	untersagt	prohibited
		verboten	forbidden

Am liebsten mache ich Wanderungen auf dem Lande.	The thing I like best is going walking in the country.
Meiner Meinung nach ist Fußball der beste Sport der Welt.	In my opinion football is the best sport in the world.
Ich treibe gern alle Sportarten außer Tennis.	I like doing all sports except tennis.

Sporting events

sich langweilen	to be bored	das Stadion	stadium
schade!	that's a shame!	unerträglich	unbearable

Letzten Samstag war ich bei einem Fußballspiel.	I went to a football match last Saturday.
Ich habe mich gelangweilt.	I was bored.
Wenn sie schneller gelaufen wären, hätten sie vielleicht gewonnen.	If they had run more quickly they would perhaps have won.
Wenn du nicht gern wanderst, solltest du lieber zu Hause bleiben.	If you don't like walks, you'd better stay at home.

Lies diesen Text und beantworte die Fragen.

Tennisschule »PRAGA«

mit VDT-Trainer Jan Holas

IN DER TENNISHALLE NEUSTADT

79822 *TITISEE – NEUSTADT Gutachstraße 37* ☎ 07651 / 2314

Hallo Tennisfreunde und solche die es werden möchten!

Tennis … längst schon kein Elitesport mehr, sondern Spiel und Spaß für jedermann. Schauen Sie doch einmal bei mir in der Tennishalle Neustadt vorbei. Es erwarten Sie 3 Hallenplätze mit gelenkschonendem Granulatboden. Oder entspannen Sie sich bei einem kühlen Drink im Tennisstühle "Mätch" und verfolgen Sie das Geschehen auf den Plätzen. Den kurzentschlossenen stelle Ich (gegen eine geringe Mietgebühr) natürlich auch Schläger und Schuhe zur Verfügung.

	a. Falsch	b. Richtig	c. Nicht im Text
1. Man muß gut Tennis spielen können, um hier zu spielen.			
2. Es gibt eine Bar in der Tennisschule.			
3. Tennisschuhe muß man haben.			
4. Es ist nicht teuer, hier zu spielen.			
5. Man kann einen Tennisschläger mieten.			

Clubs

der Beitrag (⁻e)	subscription
das Ballett	ballet
das Mitglied (-er)	member
die Veranstal-tung (-en)	(sport's) fixture

der Verein (-e)	club
teilnehmen an + Dat.	to take part in
Zeit haben	to have time

Bist du Mitglied eines Vereins?	Are you a member of a club?
Mein jüngerer Bruder ist Mitglied eines Fußballvereins.	My younger brother is a member of a football club.
Der Vereinsbeitrag ist zu teuer.	The club subscription is too expensive.
Am Wochenende nehme ich an jedem Spiel teil.	I take part in every game at weekends.
Ich gehe jeden Abend zum Jugendklub.	I go to the youth club every evening.
Letzten Samstag haben wir gegen eine Mannschaft aus Köln gespielt.	Last Saturday we played against a team from Cologne.

Holidays and activities

sich erinnern an + Akk.	to remember	**einpacken**	to pack up
sich freuen auf + Akk.	to look forward to	**organisieren**	to organize
		packen	to pack
im Urlaub sein	to be on holiday	**vorhaben**	to intend
in den Urlaub fahren	to go on holiday	**weggehen**	to go (away)
		die Pauschalreise (-n)	package tour

Ich gehe nur wenig aus, weil ich so viel Arbeit für meine Prüfungen habe.	I don't go out much because I have so much work for my exams.
Letzten Sommer bin ich in die Türkei gefahren.	Last summer I went to Turkey.
Ich habe mich so sehr auf diesen Urlaub gefreut.	I've been looking forward to this holiday so much.
Während der zwei Wochen sind wir oft zum Strand gegangen.	During the two weeks we often went to the beach.
Während wir da waren, haben wir die Ruinen besichtigt.	While we were there we visited the ruins.
Wir waren schon dreimal dort.	We've already been there three times.
Nächsten Sommer haben wir vor, wieder in die Türkei zu fahren.	Next summer we intend to go to Turkey again.
Wenn ich viel Geld hätte, würde ich nach Australien fahren.	If I had a lot of money I would go to Australia.

Preferences for going out

die Anzeige (-n)	small advert in newspaper	**sich ausruhen**	to rest
der Untertitel (-)	subtitle	**vorschlagen**	to suggest
		übersetzt	translated

Hast du heute etwas vor?	Have you got any plans for today?
Was schlägst du vor?	What do you suggest?
Sollen wir in die Stadt gehen?	Should we go to town?
Wie wäre es, wenn wir ins Kino gingen?	How would it be if we went to the cinema?
Wenn es regnet, bleibe ich lieber zu Hause.	When it rains, I prefer to stay at home.
Wenn es nicht so kalt wäre, würde ich gern schwimmen gehen.	If it wasn't so cold, I'd like to go swimming.

Money

ausgeben	to spend (money)	**verkaufen**	to sell
leihen	to borrow	**übrig**	left; remaining

Ich kann heute abend nicht ausgehen, weil ich kein Geld habe.	I can't go out this evening because I've got no money.

Ich habe mein ganzes Geld ausgegeben.	I've spent all my money.
Ich habe nur zwei Mark übrig.	I've only got two Marks left.
Ich könnte vielleicht etwas Geld von meinem Bruder leihen.	I could perhaps borrow some money from my brother.

◀ *Personal relationships and social activities* ▶

Ask permission to do things

anschalten	to switch on		**aufnehmen**	to record

Darf ich diesen Film auf Video aufnehmen?	May I record this film on video?
Fußball spielen ist hier untersagt.	It is forbidden to play football here.
Erst mit siebzehn Jahren darf man Auto fahren.	You can't drive a car until you are seventeen.
Darf man hier rauchen?	Can you smoke here?

Apologise

Verzeihung	sorry		**schuld sein**	to be one's fault
absichtlich	on purpose		**zuhören**	to listen

Es tut mir wirklich leid.	I'm really sorry.
Ich war daran schuld.	It was my fault.
Entschuldigung. Ich habe nicht richtig zugehört.	I'm sorry. I wasn't listening properly.
Das habe ich nicht absichtlich gemacht.	I didn't do it on purpose.

Discuss your problems

behandeln	to treat		**Rat geben**	to give advice
sich benehmen	to behave		**Ich habe es satt.**	I'm fed up.
besprechen	to discuss		**sich schämen**	to be ashamed
halten für + Akk.	to consider (someone) to be		**streiten**	to argue; fall out
			der/die Jugend-	adolescent
glauben	to believe		**liche (-n)**	
hindern	to prevent		**der Krach**	row
kritisieren	to criticise		**enttäuscht**	disappointed
raten	to advise		**erstaunlich**	amazing

Ich habe es satt, immer zu Hause zu bleiben.	I'm sick of always staying at home.
Ich streite oft mit meinen Eltern.	I often argue with my parents.
Meine Mutter versteht mich gar nicht.	My mother doesn't understand me at all.
Was soll ich machen?	What should I do?
Es gibt so oft Krach, wenn ich spät nach Hause komme.	There's so often a row when I come home late.
Mein Vater beschwert sich immer über meine Freunde.	My father always complains about my boyfriends.
Sie behandeln mich wie ein Kind.	They treat me like a child.

? Welcher Satz paßt zu welchem Text? Schreib den richtigen Namen in die Lücke.

In der Grundschule war ich eine der besten Schülerinnen. Aber jetzt ist es anders. Ich arbeite fleißig, aber ich vergesse immer etwas, meine Hausaufgaben, meinen Kuli oder meine Hefte. Was kann ich tun?

Anke

Zur Zeit gibt unsere Lehrerin einfach zu viele Hausaufgaben auf. Dann behauptet sie, das sei gar nicht viel. Manchmal sitzen wir zwei bis drei Stunden an den Hausaufgaben. Was sollen wir machen?

Renate

Unser Mathelehrer beurteilt unsere Leistungen nach dem Typ und nach den Noten des gesamten Zeugnisses. Er behauptet, ich sei ein 3er-Typ und würde immer eine Drei bekommen, obwohl ich in den beiden Mathetests eine Zwei geschrieben habe. Irgendwie verstehe ich das nicht. Was kann ich machen?

Trude

1 . . . . meint, daß sie zu viel zu Hause arbeiten muß.
2 . . . . meint, daß sie bessere Noten bekommen sollte.
3 . . . . hat Probleme auf der neuen Schule und vergißt immer etwas.

◄ *Arranging a meeting or activity* ►

Entertainment options

möglich   possible

Was für ein Film ist es?	What sort of film is it?
Gibt es am Samstag ein Tennisspiel?	Is there a tennis match on Saturday?
Ist es möglich, hier ins Theater zu gehen?	Is it possible to go to the theatre here?

Negotiating a meeting

ankommen   to depend on
auf + Akk.

vorschlagen   to suggest
leider   unfortunately

Ich schlage vor, daß wir uns heute abend in der Stadt treffen.	I suggest that we meet in town this evening.
Ich möchte dich lieber vor dem Kino treffen.	I'd prefer to meet you in front of the cinema.
Leider kann ich nicht so früh kommen, weil ich bis achtzehn Uhr arbeiten muß.	Unfortunately I can't come so early because I have to work until six p.m.
Das kommt darauf an.	It depends.

◀ *Leisure and entertainment* ▶

Find out what is on and when

gegen	at about	die Oper	opera

Was sollen wir am Wochenende machen?	What should we do at the weekend?
Was wird diese Woche im Theater gegeben?	What's on at the theatre this week?
Sehen wir mal in die Zeitung.	Let's look in the newspaper.
Wir könnten das Theater anrufen.	We could phone the theatre.
Die Vorstellung endet gegen dreiundzwanzig Uhr.	The performance ends at about 11p.m.

Opinions

der Erfolg	success	sich lohnen	to be worth
die Kapelle (-n)	band	wählen	to choose
die Pause (-n)	interval	entzückt	delighted
der Mörder (-)	murderer	trotz	in spite of
der Musiker (-)	musician	wegen	because of
die Rolle (-n)	role; part		

Das Konzert hat mir trotz der Musik gut gefallen.	I enjoyed the concert in spite of the music.
Der Film hat mir wegen des Hauptdarstellers nicht gut gefallen.	I didn't like the film because of the main character.
Es lohnt sich nicht, den neuen Film von Tom Cruise zu sehen.	It's not worth going to see the new Tom Cruise film.
Er hat die Rolle des Mörders gut gespielt.	He played the part of the murderer well.

The main features of a film or play

das Abenteuer	adventure	der Zauber	magic
der Angriff	attack	sich herausstellen	to turn out that
die Ähnlichkeit	similarity	suchen	to look for
der Entschluß	decision	werden	to become
die Geschichte	story	spannend	exciting
der Kampf	fight	witzig	witty
die Reise	journey	zahm	tame; friendly

Es ist ein großes Abenteuer in einer Welt voller Zauber.	It is a great adventure in a magical world.
Wie sich herausstellt, ist der Hund ganz zahm.	As it turns out the dog is quite friendly.
Es wird immer spannender.	It gets more and more exciting.

1. Für wen sind diese Filme?
2. An welchen Tagen gibt es eine Vorstellung?
3. Was kosten zwei Karten am 20. September?
4. Welcher Film handelt von einem Hund?

JUNIOR PROGRAMM
KINO FÜR KINDER

Täglich 15.15 Uhr
Einheitspreis 5,50 DM

Hallo, Kinder! Es geht wieder los. Ab 5. September starten wir wieder mit einem speziellen Programm für Euch. Täglich um 15.15 Uhr im Smoky. Am Samstag, dem 7. September, um 15.00 Uhr ist eine **Kinderparty** angesagt. Jeder Gast erhält ein kleines Geschenk und einen Bärchi-Cocktail, außerdem verlosen wir Freikarten und Filmposter. Am Freitag, dem 20. September, ist **Weltkindertag!** An diesem Tag können zwei Kinder mit einer Eintrittskarte ins „Kino für Kinder"!

Ein liebevoller Film für die ganze Familie

Wenn Kinder zu Helden und Hunde zu Sängern werden. Ein tierisches Abenteuer!

Auf Wunsch wieder bei uns.

mikey ist wieder da
und bereit, seiner größten Herausforderung ins Gesicht zu sehen: seiner kleinen Schwester.

Ein Baby kommt selten allein

Am Anfang unserer Zeit, im Land der Dinosauri...

Einsam und allein machen sich Littlefoot und seine Freunde auf die Reise ihres Lebens.

THE WORLD AROUND US

◀ *Home town, local environment and customs* ▶

Understand a description of a town or region

die Bahn (-en)	railway		die Umgebung	surroundings
die Burg (-en)	fortified castle		der Wald (¨er)	forest
das Feld (-er)	field		die Wiese (-n)	meadow
die Grenze (-n)	frontier; border		bauen	to build
die Hauptstadt (¨e)	capital		laut	noisy
der Hügel (-)	hill		riesig	huge
die Insel (-n)	island		ruhig	quiet
am Rande	at the edge		unangenehm	unpleasant
die Stimmung	mood; atmosphere			

In der Gegend gibt es schöne Berge und Wälder.	There are lovely mountains and woods in the area.
Die Stadt liegt an der Grenze zwischen Deutschland und der Schweiz.	The town lies on the border between Germany and Switzerland.
Es wurden viele neue Häuser am Stadtrand gebaut.	They've built lots of new houses on the edge of the town.
Nachts herrscht in der Stadt eine unangenehme Stimmung.	The town has an unpleasant atmosphere at night.

Your own country and others

die Aussicht (-en)	view		trocken	dry
das Einkaufs-zentrum (-zentren)	shopping centre		besser	better
der Gipfel (-)	summit		feucht	damp
die Landschaft	countryside; scenery		früher	in the past
die Landwirtschaft	agriculture		kaum	hardly
bemerken	to notice		malerisch	picturesque
scheinen	to appear		überall	everywhere

Im Winter ist es in Deutschland kälter, aber nicht so feucht wie bei uns.	In the winter in Germany it's colder but not as damp as it is here.
Es gibt mehr Industrie und es ist schmutziger.	There is more industry and it is dirtier.
Es gibt nicht so viel zu machen.	There is not so much to do.
Die Umgebung ist malerisch.	The surrounding area is picturesque.
Ich habe bemerkt, daß es viel ruhiger war.	I noticed that it was much quieter.

Where you live

anders gesagt	in other words		die Küste	coast

Was hältst du von deiner Stadt?	What do you think of your town?
Ich kann es nicht leiden, hier zu wohnen.	I can't stand living here.
Ich langweile mich zu Tode.	I'm bored to death.
Ich schäme mich, hier zu wohnen.	I'm ashamed of living here.
Man kann alles mögliche machen.	You can do all sorts of things.
Ich möchte nirgendwo anders wohnen.	I wouldn't want to live anywhere else.
Ich würde lieber auf dem Lande wohnen, weil es schöner und ruhiger ist.	I would prefer to live in the country because it's nicer and quieter.

Important festivals

das Kostüm (-e)	costume	**katholisch**	catholic
die Maske (-n)	mask	**jüdisch**	Jewish
die Moschee (-n)	mosque	**mohammedanisch**	Muslim
die Synagoge (-n)	synagogue	**zur Messe gehen**	to go to mass
evangelisch	protestant		

Was ist für dich das wichtigste Fest?	What's the most important festival for you?
Wir essen ein Festessen.	We eat a special meal.
Unsere Verwandten kommen zu uns.	Our relatives come to our house.
Wir tragen Masken und Kostüme.	We wear masks and costumes.

Weather forecasts

die Aufheiterung	brightening up	**der Wetterbericht (-e)**	weather report
der Himmel (-)	sky	**bedeckt**	overcast
die Hitze	heat	**bewölkt**	cloudy
die Höchsttemperaturen	maximum temperatures	**heiter**	bright
die Kälte	cold	**regnerisch**	rainy
die Luft	air	**teils**	partly
der Niederschlag	rain	**trüb**	overcast
der Schauer (-)	shower	**veränderlich**	changeable
die Tiefsttemperaturen	minimum temperatures	**wolkenlos**	clear (no clouds)
		hageln	to hail

Lies diese Wettervorhersage und beantworte die Fragen.

Montag	Stark bewölkt mit einzelnen Schauern.
Dienstag	Sonnig, aber ziemlich kühl.
Mittwoch	Morgennebel, später kalt.
Donnerstag	Tagsüber regnerisch und naß.
Freitag	Heiter und sonnig/trocken.

1. Du möchtest ins Freibad gehen. An welchem Tag machst du das am besten?
2. Du möchtest einen Ausflug in die Berge machen. An welchem Tag machst du das am besten?

Wie ist die Wettervorhersage für morgen früh?	What's the weather forecast for tomorrow morning?
Es sieht nach Regen aus.	It seems as if it might rain.
Morgen nachmittag wird es schön und sonnig sein.	Tomorrow afternoon it will be nice and sunny.

◀ *Finding the way* ▶

How to get to a specific place

die Ampel (-n)	traffic light	**Anlieger frei**	access only
der Bahn- übergang (¨e)	level crossing	**Ausfahrt frei halten**	do not block the exit
die Einbahn- straße (-n)	one-way street	**Bauarbeiten**	road works
		Umleitung	diversion
der Fußgänger (-)	pedestrian	**erkennen**	to recognise
die Kreuzung (-en)	crossroads	**erreichen**	to get to/to arrive at
das Parkhaus (¨er)	multi-storey car park	**kennen**	to know
Achtung!	beware!	**sich verlaufen**	to get lost

Wie komme ich am schnellsten zum Parkhaus?	What is the quickest way to the multi-storey car park?
Kennen Sie die Kirche in der Stadtmitte?	Do you know the church in the town centre?
Am besten fragen Sie beim Verkehrsamt.	It's best to ask in the tourist office.

◀ *Shopping* ▶

Finding goods and departments within a store

die Abteilung (-en)	department	**im ersten Stock**	on the first floor
der Aufzug (¨e)	lift	**im Untergeschoß**	in the basement
im Erdgeschoß	on the ground floor	**der Handschuh (-e)**	glove
die Rolltreppe (-n)	escalator	**der Regen- schirm (-e)**	umbrella
das Schaufenster (-)	shop window		
die Schreibwaren- abteilung (-en)	stationery department	**das Spielzeug**	toy (s)
Selbstbedienung	self service	**die Zahnbürste (-n)**	toothbrush

Wo ist die Kinderabteilung, bitte?	Where is the children's department, please?
Wo kann ich hier einen Regenschirm kaufen?	Where can I buy an umbrella here?
In welchem Stock kann ich Handschuhe kaufen?	On what floor can I buy gloves?

Discuss shopping habits and preferences

der Nachteil (-e)	disadvantage	**zu haben**	to be closed
der Vorteil (-e)	advantage	**hilfreich**	helpful
auf haben	to be open		

Am ersten Samstag des Monats haben alle Geschäfte am Nachmittag auf.	On the first Saturday of the month all the shops are open in the afternoon.
Ich meine, man kauft am besten bei ... ein.	I think the best place to shop is ....
Der Vorteil ist, daß es billiger ist, in so einem großen Geschäft einzukaufen.	The advantage is that it is cheaper to shop in such a large shop.

Buy or leave something

der Anzug (¨e)	suit		der Regen-	raincoat
der Badeanzug (¨e)	swimsuit		mantel (¨)	
die Badehose (-n)	swimming trunks		passen	to suit
der Gürtel (-)	belt		sich umschauen	to look around
der Hut (¨e)	hat			

Ich schaue mich nur um.	I'm only looking.
Der Anzug ist perfekt. Ich nehme ihn.	The suit is perfect. I'll take it.
Ich nehme es nicht, danke, es ist mir zu teuer.	I won't take it, thank you, it's too expensive for me.
Die Farbe steht mir nicht.	The colour doesn't suit me.
Ich möchte lieber einen Gürtel aus Leder.	I would prefer a leather belt.

Return unsatisfactory goods

ersetzen	to replace		die Quittung (-en)	receipt
funktionieren	to work		beschädigt	damaged
umtauschen	to exchange		kaputt	broken
das Loch (¨er)	hole		zerrissen	torn

Ich möchte diese Hose umtauschen.	I'd like to exchange these trousers.
Könnten Sie ihn bitte ersetzen?	Could you replace it, please?
Ich habe diesen Pulli gestern gekauft.	I bought this sweater yesterday.
Sehen Sie mal, er hat ein Loch.	Look, there's a hole in it.
Als ich ihn gekauft habe, habe ich das Loch nicht bemerkt.	When I bought it I didn't notice the hole.
Es funktioniert nicht.	It doesn't work.
Ich möchte lieber mein Geld zurück.	I would prefer to have my money back.
Ich habe die Quittung noch.	I've still got the receipt.

Explain this sign in English to your friend.

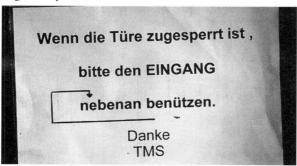

Discounts, special offers, reductions and sales

der Rabatt	discount
Sommerschlußverkauf	summer sale
Winterschlußverkauf	winter sale
10% reduziert	less 10%

Heute bieten wir zehn Prozent Rabatt auf alles Spielzeug an.	We are offering 10% discount on all toys today.

◀ *Public services* ▶

Sending letters, postcards and parcels

der Briefträger (-)	postman	die Waage	scales
das Formular (-e)	form	der Zoll	customs
die Leerung (-en)	collection (of mail)	aufgeben	to post
die Luftpost	airmail	ausfüllen	to fill in

Wieviel würde es kosten, ein Paket nach Österreich zu schicken?	How much would it cost to send a parcel to Austria?
Sie müssen für den Zoll dieses Formular ausfüllen.	You have to fill in this form for customs.
Ich habe das Formular schon ausgefüllt.	I've already filled in the form.
Legen Sie das Paket auf die Waage.	Put the parcel on the scales.
Möchten Sie es per Luftpost schicken?	Would you like to send it airmail?

Exchange money or travellers' cheques

die Kreditkarte (-n)	credit card	die Scheckkarte (-n)	bank card
der Kurs	rate of exchange	der Schein (-e)	banknote
die Münze (-n)	coin	die Wechsel- stube (-n)	exchange office
der Paß (¨sse)	passport		
der Personal- ausweis (-e)	identity card	einlösen	to cash (a cheque)
		unterschreiben	to sign
der Reisescheck (-s)	traveller's cheque	wechseln	to change (money)
der Schalter (-)	counter		

Wie ist der Kurs für das Pfund heute?	What is the rate of exchange for the pound today?
Ich möchte hundert amerikanische Dollar wechseln.	I'd like to change 100 American dollars.
Wo kann ich Reiseschecks einlösen?	Where can I change travellers' cheques?
Ich möchte nur große Scheine.	I'd just like large notes.
Kann ich Ihren Paß sehen?	May I see your passport?
Unterschreiben Sie hier, bitte.	Sign here, please.

Ask for specific coins

ein Fünfzig- pfennigstück	a fifty Pfennig coin	das Kleingeld	small change

Haben Sie ein Zehnpfennigstück? — Have you got a 10 Pfennig coin?

Report a loss or theft

die Armband-uhr (-en)	watch
die Brieftasche (-n)	wallet
der Fotoapparat (-e)	camera
das Fundbüro (-s)	lost property office
der Geldbeutel (-)	purse
die Handtasche (-n)	handbag
der Koffer (-)	suitcase
der Finderlohn	reward
die Reisetasche (-n)	hold-all; bag
die Video-kamera (-s)	video camera
liegenlassen	to leave (something behind)
stehlen	to steal
suchen	to look for
verlieren	to lose
vorgestern	the day before yesterday
überall	everywhere

Ich habe meinen Koffer verloren.	I've lost my suitcase.
Ich habe überall gesucht.	I've looked everywhere.
Mir wurde meine Brieftasche gestohlen.	Someone has stolen my wallet.
Ich habe ihn gestern verloren.	I lost it yesterday.
Ich habe ihn im Zug liegenlassen.	I left it in the train.
Können Sie den Koffer beschreiben?	Can you describe the case?
Er ist blau und ziemlich neu.	It's blue and quite new.
Was war drin?	What was in it?
Meine Schlüssel, mein ganzes Geld und meine Scheckkarte waren drin.	My keys, all my money and my cheque card were in it.
Hat es jemand gefunden?	Has anyone found it?

◀ *Getting around* ▶

Information about public transport

das Abteil (-e)	compartment
der Liegewagen (-)	couchette
das Nichtraucher-abteil (-e)	no smoking compartment
das Raucher-abteil (-e)	smoking compartment
der Schlafwagen (-)	sleeping car
der Speisewagen (-)	restaurant car (in train)
sich begeben zu	to proceed to
verpassen	to miss
Verspätung haben	to be late
statt	instead of

Ich habe meinen Zug verpaßt.	I've missed my train.
Gibt es einen Speisewagen?	Is there a restaurant car?
Ich möchte einen Platz in einem Liegewagen reservieren.	I'd like to reserve a seat in a couchette.
Achtung auf Gleis sieben!	Attention on platform seven!
Der Zug nach Bonn fährt in Kürze von Gleis fünf statt von Gleis acht ab.	The train to Bonn will shortly be leaving from platform five instead of platform eight.
Fahrgäste begeben sich bitte sofort zu Gleis fünf.	Passengers should please proceed immediately to platform five.
Der Intercity nach Dresden hat zwanzig Minuten Verspätung.	The intercity train to Dresden is running twenty minutes late.

Travel by public transport

die Fähre (-n)	ferry	**das Schiff (-e)**	ship
der Flug (¨e)	flight	**die Überfahrt (-en)**	crossing

Wann ist der nächste Flug nach London?	When is the next flight to London?

Common forms of transport

das Verkehrsmittel	means of transport	**praktisch**	practical
verschmutzen	to pollute	**reisekrank**	travel sick
ökologisch	ecological	**seekrank**	seasick

Ich fahre nicht gern mit dem Schiff, weil ich oft seekrank werde.	I don't like travelling by ship because I am often seasick.
Der Zug ist ökologischer als der Bus.	The train is more ecological than the bus.
Autos verschmutzen schrecklich die Luft.	Cars pollute the air dreadfully.

At a service station

das Benzin	petrol	**das Mofa (-s)**	moped
bleifrei	lead-free	**das Motorrad (¨er)**	motorbike
Normal	ordinary petrol	**das Öl**	oil
Selbsttanken	self service	**der Reifen (-)**	tyre
Super	top grade petrol	**der Reifendruck**	tyre pressure
volltanken	to fill up with petrol	**der Tankwart (-e)**	attendant in service station
die Autowäsche	car wash		
die Karte (-n)	map	**prüfen**	to check

Volltanken, bitte.	Fill it up, please.
Für fünfzig Mark bleifrei, bitte.	50 Marks of lead-free petrol, please.
Vierzig Liter Normal.	40 litres of ordinary grade petrol.
Ich möchte eine Karte von dieser Gegend.	I'd like a map of this area.
Nummer sieben. Was macht das?	(Pump) Number 7, what's that come to?
Könnten Sie die Reifen prüfen?	Could you check the tyres?

A breakdown

die Bremse (-n)	brake	**die Reifenpanne (-n)**	flat tyre
die Bundesstraße (-n)	main road	**die Richtung (-en)**	direction
das Geräusch (-e)	noise	**der Scheinwerfer (-)**	headlight
der LKW (Lastkraftwagen)	lorry	**eine Panne haben**	to have broken down
der Motor (-en)	engine	**reparieren**	to repair
PKW (Personenkraftwagen)	car	**komisch**	strange

Ich habe eine Panne.	I've broken down.
Können Sie einen Mechaniker schicken?	Could you send out a mechanic?

Was ist los?	What's wrong?
Die Bremsen funktionieren nicht richtig.	The brakes aren't working properly.
Es gibt ein komisches Geräusch im Motor.	There's a funny noise in the engine.
Ich bin auf der Bundesstraße Richtung Bremen.	I'm on the main road to Bremen.
Können Sie es heute reparieren?	Can you repair it today?

Report an accident

der Fahrer (-)	driver	**Straßenbauarbeiten**	roadworks
das Feuer (-)	fire	**die Versicherung**	insurance
die Feuerwehr	fire brigade	**der Wagen (-)**	vehicle
der Führer-schein (-e)	driving licence	**der Zeuge (-n)**	witness
		der Zusammenstoß	collision
der Fußgänger (-)	pedestrian	**Angst haben**	to be afraid
der Kranken-wagen (-)	ambulance	**fahren**	to drive
		fahren gegen	to bump into; to hit
die Kurve (-n)	bend	**langsamer fahren**	to slow down
der Motorrad-fahrer (-)	motorcyclist (male)	**parken**	to park
		schleudern	to skid
die Motorrad-fahrerin (-nen)	motorcyclist (female)	**überfahren**	to run over
		verletzt	injured
der Notdienst (-e)	emergency services	**versichert**	insured
die Polizei	the police	**plötzlich**	suddenly

Ein Unfall ist passiert.	There has been an accident.
Ein Auto ist gegen einen LKW gefahren.	A car has hit a lorry.
Das Auto fuhr zu schnell.	The car was going too quickly.
Er ist auf dem Glatteis ins Schleudern gekommen.	He skidded on black ice.
Wir müssen die Polizei anrufen.	We must phone the police.

1. Wann soll man 110 and 112 wählen?
2. Was kostet ein solcher Anruf?

THE WORLD OF WORK

◀ *Education and training* ▶

Information about education and training

die Berufsberatung	careers guidance	der Kurs (-e)	course
das Abitur	(roughly equivalent to) A-level	die Mittlere Reife	(roughly equivalent to) GCSE
die Fach-hochschule (-n)	college		

Wenn man Krankenschwester werden will, muß man auf die Fachhochschule gehen.	If you want to become a nurse you have to go to college.
Man muß das Abitur haben, um an der Uni zu studieren.	You have to have A-levels to study at university.

Discuss education and training

das Zeugnis (-se)	certificate	die Zukunft	future

Ich habe an der Uni studiert.	I went to university.
Ich bin seit acht Monaten Lehrling.	I've been an apprentice for eight months.
Was möchtest du in der Zukunft studieren?	What would you like to study in the future?
Ich weiß noch nicht genau, aber hoffentlich werde ich Fremdsprachen studieren.	I don't know exactly but I hope to study foreign languages.
Ich möchte eine Stelle als Friseur.	I'd like to find a job as a hairdresser.

◀ *Careers and employment* ▶

Explain choice of study or training

die Berufs-schule (-n)	technical college	die Wirtschafts-lehre	business studies

Ich möchte Wirtschaftslehre machen, weil ich gut in Mathe bin.	I would like to do business studies because I am good at Maths.
Ich möchte Geschichte studieren, weil ich das Fach gut verstehe.	I would like to study history because I understand the subject well.

Express hopes and plans for the future

sich ausruhen   to have a rest

feiern   to celebrate

Nach den Prüfungen möchte ich mich einfach ausruhen.	After the exams I just want to have a rest.
Falls ich gute Noten bekomme, möchte ich in die Oberstufe gehen.	If I get good grades, I would like to go into the sixth form.
Während der Sommerferien möchte ich etwas Geld verdienen.	During the summer holidays I'd like to earn some money.

Jobs and work experience

die Ausbildung   training
der Kassierer (-)   cashier (male)
die Kassiererin (-nen)   cashier (female)

das Vorstellungs-gespräch (-e)   job interview
anstrengend   tiring

Hast du schon mal gearbeitet?	Have you worked before?
Letzten Sommer habe ich als Kassierer gearbeitet.	Last summer I worked as a cashier.
Seit wann arbeitest du da?	How long have you been working there?
Ich arbeite seit sechs Monaten in diesem Restaurant.	I've been working in this restaurant for six months.
Es hat mir gut gefallen, dort zu arbeiten.	I enjoyed working there.

Opinions about different jobs

der Bauer   farmer (male)
die Bäuerin (-nen)   farmer (female)

im Freien   in the open air
die Chancengleich-heit   equal opportunities

Ich würde gern im Büro arbeiten, weil man da gut verdienen kann.	I'd like to work in an office because you can earn well.
Ich meine, daß das Leben eines Bauern schwer ist.	I think that a farmer's life is hard.
Die Krankenschwestern müssen sehr schwer arbeiten.	Nurses have to work very hard.
Wenn man fit werden möchte, sollte man eine Stelle im Freien suchen.	If you want to get fit you should find a job in the open air.
Wenn ich in einem Büro arbeiten würde, würde ich mich langweilen.	If I worked in an office I'd be bored.

Ist die Meinung zu diesen Arbeitsstellen positiv oder negativ?
Schreib ✓ oder ✗.

1. Ich möchte vielleicht in einem Büro arbeiten, weil die Arbeit gut bezahlt ist.
2. Obwohl man als Krankenpfleger nicht sehr gut verdient, macht das mir nicht viel aus, weil ich ger mit Leuten arbeite.
3. Obwohl man als Beamtin gut verdienen kann, würde ich die Arbeit langweilig finden.

Enquire about the availability of suitable work

feste Stelle	permanent work	**der Lohn**	wages; salary
für kurze Zeit	temporary	**Stellenangebote**	situations vacant
gesucht	wanted		

Ich suche eine Stelle als Sekretärin.	I'm looking for a job as a secretary.
Haben Sie vielleicht eine Stelle frei?	Have you perhaps got a job available?
Ich werde alles machen.	I'll do anything.
Ich bin von Anfang Juli ab frei.	I'm available from the beginning of July.
Ich habe Ihre Anzeige in der Zeitung gelesen.	I read your advert in the newspaper.
Könnten Sie mir bitte Informationen über die Stelle schicken?	Could you please send me information about the job?

Occupations

der/die Angestellte (-n)	employee	**die Geschäftsfrau (-en)**	businesswoman
der Apotheker (-)	pharmacist (male)	**der Metzger (-)**	butcher (male)
die Apothekerin (-nen)	pharmacist (female)	**die Metzgerin (-nen)**	butcher (female)
der Bäcker (-)	baker (male)	**der Soldat (-en)**	soldier (male)
die Bäckerin (-nen)	baker (female)	**die Soldatin (-nen)**	soldier (female)
der Bauarbeiter (-)	builder (male)	**der Taxifahrer (-)**	taxi driver (male)
die Bauarbeiterin (-nen)	builder (female)	**die Taxifahrerin (-nen)**	taxi driver (female)
der Geschäfts- mann (-̈er)	businessman	**der Tierarzt (-̈e)**	vet (male)
		die Tierärztin (-nen)	vet (female)

Was ist deine Mutter von Beruf?	What does your mother do as a job?
Sie ist Tierärztin.	She's a vet.
Meine Eltern sind seit sechs Monaten arbeitslos.	My parents have been unemployed for six months.

◀ *Communication* ▶

Using the phone, fax or E-mail

der Anruf- beantworter	answer phone	**das Telefon- buch (-̈er)**	telephone directory
die elektronische Post	E-mail	**abnehmen**	to pick up
etwas per Fax schicken	to send a fax	**besetzt**	engaged (phone)
		erreichen	to reach
der Telefon- anruf (-e)	telephone call	**wählen**	to dial

Bleiben Sie bitte am Apparat.	Please hold on.
Es gibt keinen Anschluß unter dieser Nummer.	The number is unobtainable.

Sie sind falsch verbunden.	You've got the wrong number.
Sie können mich telefonisch erreichen.	You can contact me by phone.
Rufen Sie mich morgen früh an,	Call me tomorrow morning
wenn Sie Zeit haben.	if you have time.

Obtain coins or a phonecard

die Einheit	unit	eine öffentliche	public telephone box
die Telefonkarte	phonecard	Fernsprechzelle	

Haben Sie einige Zehnschillingstücke	Have you got any 10-Schilling
für das Telefon?	coins for the phone?
Verkaufen Sie Telefonkarten?	Do you sell phonecards?
Zu wieviel Einheiten?	For how many units?
Zu vierzig Einheiten, bitte.	For 40 units, please.

1. Was muß man kaufen, um von dieser Telefonzelle einen Anruf zu machen?

THE INTERNATIONAL WORLD

◀ *Life in other countries and communities* ▶

Typical foods

der Aufschnitt	selection of cold meats		Salzkartoffeln	boiled potatoes
die Beilage (-n)	side dish; accompaniment		die Spezialität (-en)	speciality
			das Mehl	flour
Bratkartoffeln	fried potatoes		der Ofen	oven
der/das Gulasch	goulash		das Rezept (-e)	recipe
Plätzchen	biscuits		die Zutaten	ingredients
der Keks (-e)	biscuit		backen	to bake
der Pilz (-e)	mushroom		schlagen	to beat
			süß	sweet

Eine Spezialität dieser Gegend ist Yorkshire Pudding.	A speciality of this region is Yorkshire pudding.
Es ist nichts Süßes.	It's nothing sweet.
Man ißt es als Beilage zu Fleisch.	You eat it as an accompaniment to meat.
Man macht es aus Mehl, Salz, Eiern und Milch.	You make it with flour, salt, eggs and milk.
Man schlägt alle Zutaten zusammen.	You beat all the ingredients together.
Man läßt es zwanzig Minuten in einem sehr heißen Ofen backen.	You bake it in a very hot oven for twenty minutes.

Important social conventions

die Blume (-n)	flower		Prost!	cheers! (informal)
der Gast (¨e)	guest		zum Wohl!	cheers! (more formal)
guten Appetit!	enjoy your meal!		höflich	polite
Mahlzeit!	enjoy your meal!		schneiden	to cut

Was soll man als Gast in Deutschland machen, um höflich zu sein?	What should you do as a guest in Germany to be polite?
Man sollte das Brötchen mit einem Messer aufschneiden.	You should cut your bread roll with a knife.
Wenn man zum Essen eingeladen wird, sollte man Blumen oder Pralinen mitbringen.	If you are invited to a meal, you should bring flowers or chocolates.
Man kauft entweder fünf oder zehn Blumen, nicht zwölf.	You buy five or ten flowers, not twelve.
Guten Appetit!	Enjoy your meal!
Mahlzeit!	Enjoy your meal!

◀ *Tourism* ▶

der Berg (-e)	mountain	der See (-n)	lake
die Nebenkosten	extra costs	das Tal (¨er)	valley
das Reisebüro (-s)	travel agency	das Verkehrs-	tourist office
der Reiseleiter (-)	tourist guide (male)	amt (¨er)	
die Reiseleiterin	tourist guide (female)	irgendwann	at any time
(-nen)		irgendwo	anywhere

Haben Sie Informationen über Ausflüge in die Berge?	Have you got information on excursions into the mountains?
An welchen Tagen gibt es einen Ausflug?	On which days is there an excursion?
Sie könnten die Schlösser am Rhein besichtigen.	You could visit the castles of the Rhine.
Sind alle Nebenkosten, wie zum Beispiel Mittagessen, im Preis inbegriffen?	Are all extra costs, for example lunch, included in the price?

die Ausstel-lung (-en)	exhibition	das Eisenbahn-museum	railway museum
das Bild (-er)	picture	das Jahrhundert	century
		die Stadtmauer (-n)	city wall
		die Gegend	countryside

Was gibt es in der Gegend zu sehen?	What is there to see in the area?
Ich möchte am liebsten die alten Stadtmauern sehen.	I'd prefer to see the old city walls.
Es gibt eine schöne Ausstellung von Bildern aus dem achtzehnten Jahrhundert.	There's a nice exhibition of 18th century pictures.
Und die Gegend ist besonders malerisch.	And the countryside around is particularly picturesque.
Ich interessiere mich für das Eisenbahnmuseum.	I'm interested in the railway museum.
Ich auch.	Me, too.

Request tourist publicity

die Broschüre (-n)	brochure	die Sehens-	sight
der Camping-	campsite	würdigkeit (-en)	
platz (–e)		im voraus	in advance

Sehr geehrte Damen und Herren,

Ich habe vor, im nächsten Juli mit meiner Familie acht Tage im Schwarzwald zu verbringen.

Könnten Sie mir bitte einige Auskünfte über die Campingplätze in der Gegend schicken? Ich hätte auch gern Informationen über die Sehenswürdigkeiten der Gegend, sowie über Ausflugsmöglichkeiten.

Vielen Dank im voraus.

Mit freundlichen Grüßen

Discuss a holiday: past or future

ins Ausland fahren	to go abroad	die Katastrophe (-n)	catastrophe
das Insekt (-en)	insect	der Zweifel (-)	doubt

Wir sind nach Griechenland gefahren.	We went to Greece.
Es war wegen der Hitze und der Insekten eine Katastrophe.	It was a catastrophe because of the heat and the insects.
Am ersten Tag sind wir schwimmen gegangen.	The first day we went swimming.
Am nächsten Tag haben wir einen Ausflug zu einer kleinen Insel gemacht.	The next day we went on a trip to a small island.
Wir waren etwas enttäuscht.	We were a bit disappointed.
Wohin fahren Sie nächstes Jahr?	Where are you going next year?
Wir werden zweifellos ins Ausland fahren.	Without doubt, we'll go abroad.

Express preferences for different holidays

verbringen	to spend (time)	die Wahl	choice

Ich fahre lieber ins Ausland.	I prefer to go abroad.
Man kann sich auf gutes Wetter verlassen.	You can rely on good weather.
Ich meine, es ist besser, einen Urlaub in England zu verbringen.	I think it's better to spend a holiday in England.
Man weiß, was man zu essen bekommt.	You know what you are going to get to eat.
Man versteht die Sprache.	You can understand the language.
Wenn ich die Wahl hätte, würde ich immer ins Ausland fahren.	If I had the choice I would always go abroad.
Oft ist es billiger, als in England zu bleiben.	It's often cheaper than staying in England.
Ich wohne lieber in einer Ferienwohnung als in einem Hotel, weil man selbst das Essen zubereiten kann.	I prefer to stay in an apartment rather than a hotel because you can prepare your own meals.

◀ *Accommodation* ▶

Arrange accommodation at hotels, youth hostels and campsites

die Abreise (-n)	departure	Platz	room
die Ankunft (¨e)	arrival	der Rucksack (¨e)	rucksack
die Bettwäsche	sheets	der Schlafraum (¨e)	dormitory
der Erwachsene	adult	der Schlafsack (¨e)	sleeping bag
die Jugend- herberge (-n)	youth hostel (you often see this abbreviated to JH)	der Wohnwagen (-)	caravan
		das Zelt (-e)	tent
		leihen	to borrow
		zelten	to camp
das Kind (-er)	child	ausgebucht	fully booked

Haben Sie Platz für zwei Erwachsene und ein Kind?	Have you got room for two adults and a child?
Leider sind wir völlig ausgebucht.	Unfortunately we are fully booked.
Leider haben wir keinen Platz frei.	Unfortunately we have no room.
Wir brauchen einen Platz für ein großes Zelt.	We need a site for a big tent.
Können wir bitte Bettwäsche leihen?	Can we hire sheets?
Was kostet es pro Person und pro Tag?	What does it cost per person and per day?
Ich habe meinen eigenen Schlafsack.	I've got my own sleeping bag.
Es gibt noch Platz auf dem Campingplatz am See.	There's room in the campsite by the lake.

Rules and regulations

die Abfälle	litter	der Notfall (-̈e)	emergency
die Hausordnung	house rules	sich melden	to contact; to report to
der Herbergsvater/	youth hostel warden	verlassen	to leave
die Herbergsmutter		erlaubt	allowed
die Luftmatratze (-n)	inflatable mattress	grundsätzlich	absolutely
der Notausgang (-̈e)	emergency exit	untersagt	forbidden

Im Notfall das Gebäude sofort durch den nächsten Notausgang verlassen.	In case of emergency leave the building by the nearest exit.
Nicht mit dem Lift fahren.	Do not use the lift.
Sie müssen das Zimmer am Tag der Abreise bis 12 Uhr mittags räumen.	You must vacate the room by midday on the day of departure.
Wir bitten unsere Gäste, ab zweiundzwanzig Uhr ruhig zu sein.	Please be quiet after 10 p.m.
Rauchen ist in den Schlafräumen grundsätzlich untersagt.	Smoking is absolutely forbidden in the dormitories.
Kein Trinkwasser.	Not drinking water.
Wenn Sie Probleme haben, melden Sie sich bei dem Herbergsvater.	If you have any problems contact the warden.
Die JH wird um zweiundzwanzig Uhr dreißig abgeschlossen.	The youth hostel is locked at 22.30.

◀ *The wider world* ▶

Discuss environmental issues

das Abgas (-e)	exhaust fumes	der Umweltschutz	environmental protection
der Atom-waffentest (-s)	nuclear test	der Pazifik	Pacific Ocean
das Atom-kraftwerk (-e)	nuclear power station	die Umwelt	environment
die Bombe (-n)	bomb	die Umweltver-schmutzung	environmental pollution
das Kraftwerk (-e)	power station	der Verkehr	traffic
der Kunststoff (-e)	man-made materials	das Waldsterben	dying of the forest
die Mülltonne (-n)	dustbin	der Delphin (-e)	dolphin
die Natur	nature	der Elefant (-en)	elephant
der Naturschutz	conservation	der Walfisch (-e)	whale
das Naturschutz-gebiet (-e)	conservation area	ängstigen	to frighten
		ausschalten	to switch off
das Öko-produkt (-e)	ecologically-friendly product	schützen	to protect
der Ozean (-e)	ocean	sich Sorgen machen um + Akk.	to be worried about
der Planet (-en)	planet	gefährdet	endangered

Ich schalte das Licht aus, wenn ich aus dem Zimmer gehe.	I switch off the light when I leave the room.
Ich kaufe nur Getränke in Glasflaschen.	I only buy drinks in glass bottles.
Ich werfe meine alten Flaschen in den Sammelcontainer.	I throw my old bottles in the bottle bank.
Wir kaufen immer Umweltschutzpapier.	We always buy recycled paper.

Discuss any part of Germany you know about

demonstrieren	to demonstrate	**um**	all around
die Regierung	the government	**unzumutbar**	unacceptable

Es ist eine mittelalterliche, von einer alten Stadtmauer umgebene Stadt.	It's a medieval town surrounded by an old town wall.
An jeder Ecke findet man ein altes Gebäude.	On every corner you find an old building.
Die Regierung hat vor, eine Autobahn um die Stadt zu bauen.	The government intends to build a motorway around the town.
Die Einwohner finden das unzumutbar.	The inhabitants find that unacceptable.
Ich meine jedoch, daß es sich nicht lohnt, dagegen zu demonstrieren.	I don't think, though, that it's worth demonstrating against it.

Understand global issues

die Gefahr	danger	**die Gewalttätig-**	violence
der Müll	rubbish	**keit (-en)**	
der Regen-	rain forest	**die Hilfe**	aid; help
wald (-̈er)		**die Organisa-**	organisation
der Treibhauseffekt	the greenhouse effect	**tion (-en)**	
recyceln	recycle	**das Rassismus**	racism
schlachten	to kill; slay	**die Religion (-en)**	religion
verschmutzen	to pollute	**der Schaden (-)**	damage
umweltfeindlich	bad for the environment	**die Toleranz (-en)**	tolerance
umweltfreundlich	good for the environment	**das Verbrechen (-)**	crime
		der Verbrecher (-)	criminal
der Flüchtling (-e)	refugee	**die Wirtschaft (-en)**	economy
der Frieden	peace	**die Wohnungs-**	housing
		beschaffung	

Die Umwelt braucht Umweltschutz.	The environment needs environmental protection.
Ich mache mir große Sorgen um die Atomwaffentests im Pazifik.	I'm really worried about the nuclear testing in the Pacific Ocean.
Radfahren ist umweltfreundlicher als Autofahren.	Riding a bike is better for the environment than driving a car.
Unsere Wälder sind in Gefahr.	Our forests are in danger.
Es ist unbedingt nötig, den Regenwald zu schützen.	It is absolutely essential to protect the rain forest.

1. Was muß man mit Flaschen aus Kunststoff tun?
2. Was soll man machen, bevor man Altmetall wegwirft?

◀ *Solutions* ▶

page 5

c, f, g, h, b

page 7

1. sechs 2. Französisch 3. um 12.50 Uhr

page 10

a, b, d

page 14

zu Hause

page 17

1. Schinkenomelett mit Salat 2. Schokoeis 3. Apfelsaft

page 19

a

page 20

cycling and horse-riding

page 25

b

page 27

um 18.30 Uhr

page 31

(Man kann) Einkäufe machen.

page 32

eine Metzgerei

page 33

Am Samstag und Sonntag.

page 37

c

page 39

Nichts

page 42

DM9

page 48

1. a; 2. eine Nacht

page 54

1. Sie hat eine 4 in Geschichte; 2. b

page 57

am Mittwochnachmittag

page 63

1. a; 2. b; 3. a; 4. c; 5. b

page 66

1. Renate; 2. Trude; 3. Anke

page 68

1. für Kinder; 2. täglich;
3. DM5,50; 4. Spätzl, Frätzl & Co.

page 70

1. Freitag; 2. Dienstag

page 72

If the door is closed please use the entrance next door.

page 76

1. Wenn ein Unfall passiert ist.; 2. Nichts

page78

1. ✓; 2. ✓; 3. X

page 80

eine Telefonkarte

page 87

1. Man muß sie in den Sammelcontainer werfen.
2. Man muß es waschen/reinigen.